ALL THAT GLITTERS IS NOT God

ALL THAT GLITTERS IS NOT God

Breaking Free from the Sweet Deceit of Multi-Level Marketing

Athena Dean
Author of **Consumed by Success**

WINEPRESS WP PUBLISHING

Published by WinePress Publishing, PO Box 1406, Mukilteo, WA 98275
Cover design by HoweDesign, Ft. Collins, CO

ISBN 1-57921-134-8

To my children: **Garrett**, **Aaron**, **Roby**, and **Ailen**. They are the lasting fruit of my decision to walk away from the multi-level lifestyle. When I wrote my first book, *Consumed by Success*, they were bitter and backslidden. Now, three years later, they are all—that's right, every one of them—radically saved, on-fire, Spirit-filled, totally committed, unwilling-to-compromise, fruit-producing believers. What a privilege it is to serve such an awesome God shoulder to shoulder with my children.

To my husband, **Chuck**, who stands by me through all the flack, persecution, and controversy that inevitably comes as I persist in exposing the dark side of multi-level marketing. I know being married to me has not always been easy. Your support and encouragement has made it easier to take the hits. I love you.

And to my **Heavenly Father**, Who has changed my heart so much in the last four years. I may take the credit for getting this message into print, but He gets all the glory.

Contents

Introduction

For years I was consumed with money, prestige, and recognition, even as a Spirit-filled Christian! As a result, I ended up with broken relationships and a fractured family life. I also found myself in a serious spiritual drought. But it's different now. I'm different. Life is certainly different. I made a choice—one could say a *redecision*. I chose to break free from the sweet deceit that had marked much of my adult life and consumed my soul.

As a result of my choice, I now enjoy and treasure restored relationships built on the new, pure motives of my heart. I have a renewed family life, full of depth and rich with meaning and purpose. But most of all, I have a totally renewed relationship with my loving Heavenly Father.

There's no question in my mind whatsoever: I made the right choice.

Before I made the choice, I was blind to anything but the glitter of unrealistic dreams and elusive goals. I couldn't see the destruction or the pain my ambition caused my husband. Neither could I see the heartbreak of my children. All I could see was the way to make more money, recruit more people, and achieve another award. I let the glitter appeal to my senses and lead me down an exciting, dangerous road toward spiritual death. I was consumed by success.

But then, one day, I was forced to face a moment of truth. And the truth that was forced upon me was simply this: All that glitters is *not* God. Somewhere I had made a wrong turn, a life-changing choice based on deceit—the very sweet deceit of multi-level marketing (MLM). And in that moment of truth I knew no matter what it cost, no matter how painful, I wanted out.

But it wasn't easy. Breaking free from the mindset of the unhealthy pursuit of success at any cost came with a price. I had to be willing to totally overhaul the values I held and the way I viewed life. I had to face the fact that I didn't know what was best or even right anymore. I was forced to admit that only God's will for my life was worth pursuing. Only His character being re-created in me was worth my all-consuming passion.

"That's not what happened to me," you say.

Perhaps not. But how can you be so sure? My first book, *Consumed by Success*, opened the eyes of many involved in MLM. Letters and e-mail messages by the score have crossed my desk in the two years since the first publication of my book. But opening eyes isn't enough for me anymore. Simply to help a person see that she's made a mistake and that she needs to change doesn't do it. Those caught in the same sweet deceit of MLM that I was in need more. They need a step-by-step guideline and lots of checklists to mark their progress.

Still not sure if you need this book and its message? Then ask yourself the following:

1. Do you spend so much time each day thinking about your business that you have very little time left to spend in quietness with the Lord?

2. Do you view people in general—friends, family, and acquaintances—as a means to an end (i.e., your success in business)?
3. Do you react to the negative comments about your product or opportunity as an evil scheme from the devil to steal your dream?
4. Do you believe your opportunity to be the best way for anyone who wants to earn extra money to fulfill that desire?
5. Are you more excited, animated, talkative, and enthusiastic about your opportunity than you are talking to a friend about Christ?
6. Do you find yourself fellowshipping exclusively with those who are involved and/or positive about your business?
7. Do you see your opportunity as the only way to escape the bondage of a typical nine-to-five job?
8. Do your current role models focus mostly on the big incomes, nice houses, new cars, annual vacations, and financial independence?
9. Do you tend to concentrate your time on relationships that help you build your business, and neglect those who don't?
10. Do you justify pouring your time, energy, and resources into your business now because it will pay off later?

If you answered yes to more than four of these questions, you are already trapped in the web woven by the sweet deceit of multi-level marketing. But you don't have to stay that way. You can change. You can get free from the deception and its seductive entanglement.

This book has been written just for you. It will not judge you, nor will you find condemnation in its pages. No one knows more than I do on how the deception works. I've experienced firsthand the devastating results.

The following pages are designed to help you identify the areas of your life that are not yet completely yielded to the Lord. The questions are intended to give you hope that you can again live in the center of God's perfect will. This message may rip the glitter from your heart, but you will find that behind the glitter beats a heart for God. You are about to step into the freedom that comes from knowing and facing the truth.

Every phase of the devious MLM practices will be explored and exposed. You will find ways to resist the enticement. I'll show you how to unwind the tentacles of deception that are pulling you into a plan that opposes God's best for your life.

Ready? Let's begin with the approach.

PART ONE:
THE SWEET DECEIT

The Approach

Multi-level marketing has invaded the church. In every denomination people just like you are targeted each week. Perhaps you have been approached by a "brother" or "sister" who will befriend you, shower you with Christian love, and tell you how successful and what a winner you are—or could be. Eventually they ask if you have ever considered supplementing your income. They might even ask if you are unhappy at your job. Finally, they will inquire if you might be interested in seeing a "Christian" business opportunity. You might be told someone in the area is looking to increase his or her business. Rather than go through traditional channels, they are hoping that through word of mouth they will find exactly the right Christian individuals to add to their business. Time is of the essence, of course, and they lead you to believe that astute individuals will recognize the hand of the Lord in this opportunity and move without delay.

"We met them at church," Leona said. "They seemed like a nice couple. We introduced ourselves and soon began to socialize together. We had them over for dinner, and our families seemed to click right off."

"They didn't approach us until about six months later," her husband joined in. "And even then it was so subtle."

"Soft sell?" I asked.

"No way," Leona said. "A soft sell is a lot more up front than that. Like Larry said," she nodded toward her husband, "it was so subtle."

"Once I figured out what they were up to," Larry said, "I made it clear that we were not interested. The relationship cooled dramatically after that."

"Did you back away?" I asked.

"Oh, no," she said. "Not us—them."

"Sad thing is," Larry added, "the same thing happened to many other couples in our church. I guess they didn't get many takers, because they soon left our church for another one nearby."

"Nearby? Did they go to a church of a different denomination?" I asked.

"I got the feeling that denominational loyalty wasn't a priority. They were fishing, but our church wasn't stocked with hungry fish, so they moved on to fish in another pond."

Sound familiar? Not every person who is approached escapes as easily as Larry and Leona. I know I didn't.

Not long after Chuck and I were married, a friend approached us asking for our opinion of a new business venture he was getting into. Who wouldn't want to help a friend make a big decision like that? Flattered and feeling important, we attended an informational meeting, just to be another set of eyes and ears for him.

I told the story in my first book.

Chuck and I walked into a darkened room where a video of an old *Phil Donahue* program was playing. Donahue was exposing corrupt practices in the insurance industry, the same industry that this new business was going up against. After the video was over, a down-to-earth man in his forties got up and very eloquently embellished the crusade. He spoke of the common-sense ideas that would help people make and save money. These sound, financial principles had been hidden from the average American family by the greedy insurance and banking industries. The "wrong" that was being perpetrated on innocent consumers quickly began to draw us in.

The speaker skillfully painted a verbal picture of the "deception of the corporate dream." Like an expert craftsman he began to weave a blanket of discontent that subtly covered the standard idea of working nine to five. Ever so smoothly he spread his net of doubt about working for a paycheck of limited potential and questioned the security of benefits that may or may not be there later when you really needed them.

The opportunity he outlined really seemed like something that genuinely offered financial independence. If a person simply put in enough effort and worked hard to build his business initially, soon he would be able to back off and enjoy life while the business continued to generate income.[1]

Somehow we forgot that we were there to be the eyes and ears for our friend asking our advice—we wanted in! Without really knowing it, we opened the door to one of the most common approaches to the sweetest deceit ever: multi-level marketing. Our friend wasn't interested in what we thought of the idea. He wanted us approached by the idea firsthand.

So what kind of people are we? Gullible, lazy, or dumb? On the contrary, we are intelligent, hard-working, and savvy people who just want a piece of the American Dream. We are not so different from those who, for the most part, live right next door or go to our churches and who are trying hard to get ahead.

And we're exactly like millions of others who get approached by MLMers every day of every month each year.

Recently a lady from Colorado wrote me.

I read the article you wrote in *Charisma* magazine ["Escape from Greed," June 1997] and felt I had to write.

Just this past weekend my family and I fell victim to this ungodly and deceptive ploy by someone in our church. We, like some people you mentioned in your article, have been hoping for some fellowship within our church. When this woman we barely knew expressed a deep interest in getting to know us, we were surprised but delighted. She invited us, along with others from a class at church, to a "fellowship" gathering/birthday party for her little girl. I gave her my address. A few days after receiving her invitation, I also received a mailer about a product line she was involved in. A little bell went off for me, but I gave her the benefit of the doubt and forgot about it. When we got to the party, her purpose in inviting all of us soon became clear: to become part of her business or at least buy some products. As soon as I realized this (just prior to the presentation), I took my family and politely left. I was disappointed and hurt.

I had spent time shopping for a gift for a child I barely knew and made my family go out after church when we were tired from a full morning of teaching Sunday school and a weekend full of real ministry. I felt bad for the other folks still back at the party, who were forced to endure a merciless sales pitch after being promised fellowship.

I've had it with multi-level marketing. You see, I was one while dating my husband and prior to coming to the Lord. It almost destroyed our relationship, and we got out before it was too late. I'll never be taken in again.

It wouldn't be so bad, but this is the third time in a year and a half that someone at my church has attempted to draw us in under the guise of fellowship or by appearing to serve a need.

I thank you for your article and intend to keep photocopies of it on hand for the next person who tries to seduce me under the guise of friendship. Let's just pray that more of God's people finally see the light.

MLM isn't new, but it does get more subtle with each new approach. MLM techniques are often deceptive in nature. The approach is only the beginning. Each successive level of involvement in MLM is completely saturated with hidden agendas. The plan not only includes you but all your friends, your family, and especially your fellow believers. How will they be approached? Through you. You will deliver the approach next time. And where will you make the approach? If you're a church attender, can you think of a better, more convenient place?

You might ask, "What's wrong with that?" Very simply, the church is supposed to be a safe place for us to have relationships with others, to be family, to be nurtured and protected from abuse. When church becomes the place where we solicit and sell our wares and opportunities, it becomes a place of merchandise rather than a house of prayer. It is no longer a safe place.

Each approach is a little different. The kinds of approaches are limited only by the creative ability of the *upliners* (those above you who earn commissions on the sales you and your group make) in the organization. See if you can remember being approached in any of these ways.

What You See Is Not What You Get

MLM simply denies that it is an MLM. Instead, it claims to be a personal retail network or distinguished *downline* distribution company or some other such non-MLM-sounding organization. However, remember the old adage: If it walks like a duck, talks like a duck, smells like a duck . . .

I said it in my first book, and I'll say it again: If you have to recruit distributors in order to make the big money, it's definitely some form of multi-level marketing, no matter what name it is being called.[2]

I Need Your Advice

This approach is overtly deceptive at the onset. Chuck and I believed it once. We even used this approach ourselves. However, remember this: Giving someone the benefit of your wisdom and insight shouldn't cost you in any way. Giving your opinion should not lead to a financial investment or having your life turned upside down like it did for us.

Let's Party!

The homey, party atmosphere is exploited as your friend invites you over for a fun time of fellowship and to view a new line of products. You don't mind attending, because if she has enough people show up and buy, your friend wins free product for being a good hostess. This approach seems harmless, but when guilt and subtle pressure are used to get people to buy, many end up feeling abused in this setting. Often attendees are expected to buy without checking with their spouses or budget first. Snap decisions affected by the peer pressure keep excitement at an all-time high and sales rolling in.

Guess Who's Coming to Dinner?

In this technique, people are invited over for dinner and fellowship. Toward the end of a pleasant evening, a "business associate" of the host conveniently drops by to help recruit the unsuspecting dinner guests. Manipulative and potentially hazardous to friendships, this is one of the most effective approaches used and abused.

The Incredible Ground-Floor Business Opportunity

You're invited to a house or to lunch for "the discussion." Very similar to What You See Is Not What You Get, this approach lets you know up front that it's a business and it will probably require that you work at it. You will probably be invited to invest your time and your money.

What isn't disclosed at the beginning is the fact that you will have to aggressively build your downline to feed the insatiable hunger of your upline. What you don't see is that those on the bottom level are doomed to lose, unless of course they can dupe someone else into coming in on the ground level, who will dupe someone else, who will dupe someone else. . . .

Friendship Farming

You intentionally pick out someone who looks sharp at a little league game, soccer game, church fellowship time, PTA meeting, etc. You strike up a conversation, asking questions such as: How long have you lived in the area? How many kids do you have? Has your kid been in soccer long? What kind of work do you do? Sooner or later they will ask, "What do you do?" That's exactly what you want to hear so you can recruit them by having *them* ask *you!* It is intentional friend making with a hidden agenda. The idea is, if you ask them to talk about themselves for long enough, sooner or later they'll ask you about yourself. By then, if you've asked them how they like their job and have gotten any negative feedback, you have all the buttons to push when you start describing your opportunity!

Who Do You Know?

When I was involved in MLM we used a campaign that challenged us to ask twenty people per day, "Who do you know?" It went like this: If you went up to someone and said, "You look like someone who would like to earn an extra $500 to $1,000 a month part time," he would be offended and defensive. If you went up to that same person, however, and said, "Hey, I'm sure you wouldn't be interested, but do you know anyone who could use an extra $500 to $1,000 a month part time?"

Usually they'd say, "Well, what about me?"

You're not really interested in whom they know. You want to interest them, but by asking, "Who do you know?" This way you'll evoke more interest. This manipulative behavior is common in MLM.

The "Ask Me" Button

Many organizations give out buttons that read: "I lost _____ lbs. Ask me how." You fill in the blank and walk around just waiting for people to inquire. Once they do, you have an open invitation to pitch an informational meeting about the product. Not just a sales pitch, mind you, but one that hopefully ends up snagging a recruit.

———— ⌘ ————

Whatever manipulation is used to get you there, the goal of the approach is the same: to help you suspend common sense and good judgment long enough to entice you with the allure. Without even so much as batting an eye, Chuck and I fell for the approach of network marketing. Ever so gently, the sweet deceit of multi-level marketing began its devious and ultimately devastating work in our lives. Because we became convinced that the dream of financial independence through MLM was real, we justified that all the approaches I've just shared with you were a fair means to introduce people to the opportunity. The fact that many of the approaches were outright deceit never occurred to me, because I was so sure that my opportunity was *for everyone* and that it was *from God.*

If someone had only warned us and told us to be on our guard, things could have been far different. Sadly, there was no book to warn us of the dangerous days ahead. There was no watchman on the wall to sound the alarm. But that's all changed now. You're holding the very book we needed. This book is that alarm. You are being warned.

Think about it: Have you been showered with love lately by someone (even a Christian brother or sister) who shows more than an average interest or concern in your financial situation? Has a "friend" shown an exceptional appreciation for the fact that you could be wasting your talent and effort in what he considers a dead-end job or a job with limited potential? Have you been encouraged to think beyond your present means, to dreams of financial independence and improved social status? Can you recall recent conversations about some intriguing opportunity with only vague answers given to your questions about the actual business, product, or investment required?

Have you been invited for a social occasion, only to find out that your hosts used the evening to present their most exciting opportunity ever? Have you noticed some believers using church fellowship activities to approach others?

If you answered yes to any of the above questions, you will have to admit that, as much as we'd like to pretend otherwise, the MLM approach is alive and well. And, like it or not, it has come to church.

Here are some effective strategies that will help you escape being snared by the MLM approach.

How to Protect Yourself

1. *Be vigilant.* MLM is out there, and your church probably has many who are loyal and dedicated to the idea. They are committed to getting you in on the ground level—the level just beneath them, of course, or somewhere else in their downline. They would like nothing more than to profit from your relationship. Certainly not every relationship has such hidden agendas woven into their very fabric. But enough do that we must establish our relationships on real love and a tight bond in Christ that will not allow deceptive business approaches in.

2. *Be courageous.* If someone asks you to his or her home and then switches from Christian fellowship to an MLM approach, be ready to confront if necessary. Leave if you have to. You're not really risking a friendship, because friendships have no hidden agendas. Get out while the getting is good. Make it your personal policy to keep friends as friends, not as a potential sales force.

3. *Be merciful.* Keep in mind that the person approaching you believes he is doing you a favor. He sincerely believes that he is helping you or at least offering you a wonderful opportunity. Remember, in his eyes he is not wrong. He is sold on the misbelief that he is giving you the very best thing next to salvation itself. Be polite in your mercy while being firm in your resistance.

4. *Be smart and ask lots of questions.* Be specific in your questions. Ask for and expect specific answers. If you are tempted to get involved with MLM, keep asking questions about the product and why it can't be bought through regular channels. Ask how many levels are already in the company. How many middlemen does it take to bring a quality product to market? Finally don't be afraid to ask, "Who are these guys?" Then ask the state attorney general's office or the Better Business Bureau. Everybody leaves some kind of track. Find out their track record. What is the focus of the company: product, or opportunity?

5. *Use common sense.* Is network marketing really the best way for a consumer to make necessary purchases? If so, why do major corporations spend millions on advertising? When was the last time you saw the product being sold by your MLM advertised in usual consumer magazines? If the product was so wonderful, why is it so hard to get? Take a sample to a traditional marketplace, supermarket, or natural food store to compare. If the price seems out of line, ask why.

6. *Take responsibility for yourself.* Who will protect you from the approach of the MLMers in your town, neighborhood, and church? You will. It's time you realize that neither the government nor the church can look out for you. You will have to put in place these and other strategies to guard yourself, your family, and your future from MLM. You'll have to begin right here by resisting the approach. Otherwise, you'll have to find the strength to resist the allure.

2

The Allure

"About a year ago," Greg wrote, "I was introduced to an 'opportunity.' It seemed like something that could really give me financial independence. I'd spend time working hard to build the business, then I'd be able to do what I pleased while 'the business' continued to generate income on its own.

"As I listened to the full business presentation," he continued, "feelings of discontentment grew. The more I thought about my nine-to-five paycheck, the more discontent I felt. I began to ask myself questions like, *Do you think your company is really looking out for you?* My mind was literally reeling. *What could I do with an extra $1,000 or $1,500 each month? Hey, I could buy a new car, work toward retirement savings, move to a bigger house. I could* *become financially independent. Maybe even work from home and have more time with the kids."*

What Greg didn't realize was that he was buying into the *allure*—the second level of involvement in multi-level marketing. Later, Greg admitted, "I didn't even see it coming. Discontentment's partner, Greed, walked right in and took center stage." He didn't know that he wasn't just buying into the business of selling long-distance telephone service; he was opening the door to the buying and selling of friends and family and was willing to spend his precious after-work hours and energy to do it. Furthermore, it wasn't just a long-distance business he was being exposed to but the much larger, more tempting business machine of MLM.

Following the approach comes the first meeting, dinner invitation, or party where the allure is carefully planned. The product isn't the real issue here, for it could be cosmetics, health aids, household cleaners, reference books, and even recordings. One MLM even sold its recruits the right to collect money for destitute children—that's right, a charity! While everyone took a healthy cut of the proceeds, the needy children got very little. (That Christian MLM is no longer in business.)

How does it happen? First the approach, then the allure. At the initial or informational meeting, the product is very much in the forefront. The potential recruit is met by gaily colored bottles of fingernail polish, attractively arranged product displays, professionally prepared customer catalogs, and the like. But the ordinary customer knows that she can buy good quality cosmetics, skin-care products, and vitamins off the shelf. The product alone isn't the allure; it's the promises mixed with the products that become almost irresistible.

> Set your own hours! Be your own boss! Double your income! Make more money than you ever dreamed! Work around your present job. Increase your spendable cash in your spare time. No experience needed.

The allure sounds so wonderful. If your informational meeting also includes slide or video presentations, notice how much the benefit of building an organization that sells the product is inter-woven with the benefit of the product. You no longer think just in terms of selling the product and getting customers. You begin to wonder whom you can get to sell the product and whom they can get to sell the product. You're already beginning to think not single-level marketing—but multi-level!

You may have come to learn about building a plastic-container, party plan business, but soon you feel almost intoxicated with the promises of fellowship, fulfillment, independence, and escape from the cruel corporate world that cares nothing about you. The allure is very strong and extremely attractive. It is irresistible to many who haven't resisted the approach.

"We didn't sign up right away," Pam said. "We went to several meetings first. But we were remodeling our house, and it was get-ting very expensive. We needed extra money. Finally, we signed up. Even though they didn't make us specific promises, we were lured by the way the tapes and books promoted the idea of becoming independently wealthy. Hey, when you've struggled just to make ends meet, pictures of people enjoying luxurious vacations and beautiful clothes—it just turned our heads."

This is exactly what the allure is supposed to do. It is designed to be tempting, enticing, and emotionally seductive. It tantalizes you with hope by inviting you to think beyond your present, diffi-cult, or at least boring circumstances and arouses your appetite for something more exciting. The basic human fascination with wealth and the magnetic pull of riches are as old as human nature itself. Appealing to our sense of "life isn't fair," extra income and spare-time riches become more than attractive. After all, it's how the home-office and upline folks manage to keep their wealth coming in. Why wouldn't they invest in first-rate video presentations and full-color brochures? You see, they're not really selling you on their way of life; they're selling the idea, the dream of their way of life. That's how they support it in the first place.

So you've been approached, and now you've been exposed to the allure. How can you possibly resist?

What's Right about MLM

Coming from your first meeting, you can honestly have a very positive feeling about the meeting, the group, and the company. After all, some things are right about MLM. For example, the product is often very right. Even an MLM wouldn't get very far with a shoddy product—although some have in the past. What's more, MLM recruitment meetings introduce you to one of the most intense sensations of being welcome, promising you a secure place to belong. Some meetings even feel like church! Of course, there's always plenty of recognition for a job well done. Plaques, watches, pins, and bonus checks all sweeten the allure. There is even some truth to the potential financial independence and financial freedom. A few people really do make big money, go from rags to riches, and make their material dreams come true without a college education or formal training.

In addition to all that, MLM meetings are usually charged with an electric atmosphere where people are encouraged to excel. Competition is played down; and the contrast from the day-to-day, dog-eat-dog corporate world is refreshing. Your personal growth and a positive self-image are boosted each time you attend. Couples find they can work together and have more time together. Shy people often break through their shyness into a boldness they only dreamed about before. Let's face it, MLM meetings, conferences, and rallies give people hope and confidence. And for the moment, that's a big plus in what many deem to be a hopeless world.

Our MLM meetings were always so exciting! We set the lighting just right and put out fewer chairs than we knew we would need. It's always more exciting to have to pull out more chairs because so many people are coming to the meetings! Chuck and I always presented an "up" image for the meetings, even if we fought all the way there.

What is not right about MLM is the allure—the bait. Sadly for many, buried deep within that tempting, alluring dream is a sharp and deadly hook. You might enjoy the fantasies for a while, but once you sign up, the hook is set and it goes deep.

Believe me, I know what it's like to feel the strong, magnetic tug of the allure. When Chuck and I attended our first recruitment meeting, our current business felt like a ball and chain around our necks. What was presented to us that night seemed like it could really give us some financial independence. We would spend time working hard to build the business and eventually be able to do what we pleased while it continued to generate income. The allure for Chuck and I was definitely the residual income. Hearing that all we had to do was work hard for five years and then never have to work again did it! When we eagerly signed up and made our initial investment, we had no idea we swallowed the hook. How many of us former MLMers have uttered the words, "If I had only known then what I know now."

But it doesn't have to be that way for you. Perhaps you've been approached. "Hey!" you say to yourself, "this sounds good to me! Guess I'll look into this. After all, my friend says it's a good deal, and he wouldn't mislead me, would he?" But now you're reading this book. Suddenly you're not so sure. Maybe you'd like to bail out now, before you swallow the hook. There is a way to defend yourself against the allure.

Defensive Measures and Strategies

If you're one of those people who have responded to the approach, flirted with the allure, but are now hesitant, wouldn't you like to know what you should look for and how you can resist until you can make a firm, solid, rational decision? Consider the following:

- Does it seem too good to be true?
- Are you *feeling* like this is an answer to prayer?
- Does it "seem right" and appear to make total sense, even if you don't fully understand it?
- Has it been presented as a cure-all for your problems and financial difficulties?
- Are big incomes, vacations in exotic locations, and nice cars and houses interspersed in the presentation, brochures,

videos, or audio tapes with good wholesome hot buttons—such as spending more time with your family, being your own boss, and being able to give to ministries and church building programs?

If you answered yes to any of the above questions, then beware. We justify in our minds that the good and wholesome things make all the other carnal things excusable. But sooner or later the lust of the flesh, the lust of the eyes, and the pride of life take over. The carnal things become our desire as much as if not more than the wholesome things!

Again, beware. Satan himself masquerades as an angel of light (2 Cor. 11:14). Remember, God's ways are not our ways! (See Isa. 55:8–9.) Just because a door is open doesn't mean God wants us to walk through it! Just because it glitters doesn't mean that God is in it. Proverbs 14:12 says, "There is a way that seems right to a man, but in the end it leads to death."

Your best defense and strategy at this point? Just say no and mean it. You need extra income? Get another job, cut expenses, or see a nonprofit financial or credit counselor. But to continue on—to swallow the hook—means you will just get into a fix you tried to fix your present fix with. Confusing? This is nothing. Swallow the hook, you'll see.

But I'm Already In!

"I've already been sucked in," you say. "Right now I'm doing a bottom-of-the-totem-pole business and am thinking about recruiting. After all, I've been told I can make money doing this. I've already paid my money. Guess I might as well go whole hog. How can I withstand the allure of building my own downline?"

If you really want to keep your motives pure, make some decisions up front.

1. Never approach your friends and family.
2. Church members and leadership are off limits.

3. Build your business by selling a good product for a fair price to those who are looking for your product. In other words, advertise your product in the phone book or in local newspapers and respond to those who call you. Do not aggressively solicit people you know or meet for business. Get exposure for your product, and allow the Lord to send you customers.

4. When you do approach people to build your downline, be completely honest. Tell them exactly what you want and what you are doing, without any deception or manipulation. If it really is of God, you will have success without hiding the truth or doing a bait and switch.

If you can't do any of these, then get out. Sell off what product you have left at the nearest flea market, store it in your garage, or throw it away. This is your life we're talking about here, not merchandise. What does the Bible say? "What good is it for a man to gain the whole world, yet forfeit his soul?" (Mark 8:36). Do you think your soul isn't at stake here? Sadly, many don't see it that way, but it is.

I've Been In a While, and Lately . . .

". . . there's a nagging something or other lying like a rock at the pit of my stomach. Could I have been wrong to get in this deep? I believed the allure; is there help for me? I'm not making a ton of money yet; but if I gave up coaching Little League, I'd have a few more hours each week. My kids would understand."

1. *Face the truth.* That nagging feeling is the Holy Spirit trying to get your attention. He has been trying for a long time now, but you've wanted to believe the dream; you've wanted it to be from God. It's not. Face the facts.

2. *Quit trying to make it work.* Another two hours a week won't make the difference. Be willing to admit that you made a mistake.

3. Cut your losses now and begin to mend all the relationships you've blown because you approached your friends and family with your MLM.

Save Your Breath . . .

". . . I got in early, and I'm making baskets full of money. OK, I've mostly dropped out of church. But hey, I still believe in God and everything. Besides we have church services at the motivational conferences I attend most weekends. It's not that important *where* I worship but that I do worship somewhere. Anyway, I'm so close to going to the top management level that it'll be only a few more months and then I can sit back, relax, and let the money come to me. What could you possibly say to me? I listened to the approach, swallowed the allure, and it's about to pay off big time!"

1. I repeat: What does it profit a man if he gains the whole world and loses his own soul?
2. Don't kid yourself. You'll never be able to sit back and relax. You'll always have to keep motivating the troops to bring in new people; otherwise, your income will inevitably drop.
3. You may have changed the *place* you worship, but are you so sure you haven't also changed *who* and *what* you worship?
4. Face it, you'll never be satisfied no matter how much money you make and all the good things you do with it. The only thing that will satisfy you is a deep, intimate relationship with the living God. Your MLM lifestyle serves as a barrier between you and Him. Are you sure it's worth the trade off?

So why don't people resist the allure, even if they've responded to the approach? Because MLM traffics in sweet deceit. Do you think the people realize they're being deceived? Of course not. Do you think the person recruiting you knows he is leading you into deception? Certainly not. He honestly thinks he is offering you a genuine opportunity. If the deception was exposed and brought into the open,

MLM would fold. It would all come crashing down at once. MLM depends on deception. That's why it's offered so highly sweetened with promises of dreams that exist for only a very few. But people by the score still answer the seductive beckoning of the approach and allow themselves to be tempted by the dreamy allure. Once they bite—ouch! There's a hook buried in that allure that goes deep into the mouth of the unsuspecting recruit. A hook that sets so deep it's almost impossible to get out without damage being done.

The Hook

Since *Consumed by Success* was published, I've written several articles for leading Christian magazines. The responses continue to come to my office. Letters and e-mail, faxes and phone calls have come from people who want my book not to be true—or at least not for them.

Dear Athena:

I am a mother of two young children and in need of supplementing our income while staying at home and looking after them. I responded to an ad in a Christian magazine that turned out to be an MLM. It seems like the ideal thing to me. I love the Lord, and my utmost desire is to fulfill His purpose and my destiny. *But* I also want to get out of the rut. I want to be financially independent, experience a breakthrough in my finances, and stay out of debt. At the same time, I want to maintain my relationship with God and not get off the track. In other words, I want to be rich but also remain a child of God and fulfill God's plans for my life.

I've been praying for God's direction for about three years. I still want His will, but I want the other too. Is it possible to be an MLM associate and not fall into the trap of covetousness or misplacement of priority?

Possible? Perhaps. Probable? Not likely. In all likelihood our young mother hasn't faced or hasn't even been told the whole truth. New and prospective recruits are seldom told the downside of the business. Prospective recruits are rarely told six important facts that will keep them from taking the alluring bait and swallowing the hook.

1. How much time will it actually take to become successful in MLM?
2. What are their chances of becoming successful even if they spend all their spare time and extraordinary energy on working the plan?
3. How much money will they have to invest before they realize even a modest income?
4. How much effort will they actually have to expend?
5. How much rejection and humiliation will they have to endure while building their downline?
6. How many friends or family members might they lose along the way?

I wonder how Greg would answer our young mother about to swallow the hook, complete with line and sinker. Writing about his own experience in MLM, Greg said:

None of the formal business presentations I attended ever said it, but I eventually learned from intensified training to use my personal relationships, my credibility, and my resources to make this business happen. I was totally convinced that I was helping my friends. But then reality set in:

"Daddy, I never get to spend time with you anymore. . . ."

"Greg, you're always on the phone talking about . . ."

I was so intense. I rationalized that my wife and family just didn't understand. I only intended to build the business enough to create the momentum I needed to back away and let the energy I spent pay off. Then I'd have the time I wanted to kick back and be with them. Right. I believed the lie. But after five years I realized that day wasn't any closer to coming now than ever before. I worked hard to build one level, then even before I started to enjoy the freedom, I dug back in and worked even harder to reach the next level. The cycle never stopped. As much as I hate to admit it now, my human nature wanted more, bigger, better, faster things to keep it fueled. Financial freedom, once my goal, had become my *master.*

Greg had embraced the allure and swallowed the hook. It's true: In order to make it big in MLM you must eat it, sleep it, live it, breathe it. Building your business must consume you, your life, and your thoughts. You must give it your whole heart, mind, soul, and strength. After all, you've been told you're a *winner.* Only losers do less, and they fail.

In 1991, when I got involved for the second time in MLM (this time as a born-again believer), I found myself justifying my workaholic tendencies with Ecclesiastes 9:10, "Whatever your hand finds to do, do it with all your might." I told myself nothing good comes without a fight, so I have to be committed to excellence and hard work. I have to be a good example for those below me, especially if I want to make a decent income off their production! I found myself always thinking about how to build my organization bigger, how to find more people, how to present the business in a way that people would accept, how to start a new contest to spur additional sales. My mind never turned off the business. I truly did live it, breath it, eat it, sleep it. And yes, I did make it big in MLM, making over $20,000 a month. I gave those below me—who did not make it big—hope and caused them to be committed to eating it, breathing it, sleeping it, and living it just like I did. The truth is, I taught other Christians to live a life of idolatry. I taught other believers to love the product and opportunity with all their hearts, minds, souls, and strength—not the Lord their God, as the Scripture commands!

Unbaiting the Hook

No fish in his right mind would bite an unbaited hook, right? Without the allure, there would be no catch of the day. Let's take a closer look at some of the appealing allures and see the actual hook hidden inside.

ALLURE: Because of the business, you can become financially independent and have freedom. You will have to work only five years or so and never have to work again. The residual income will come in for life!

HOOK: Once you swallow that lure you will be hooked. Those who make the big money in MLM must build their downlines over and over again. You will have to keep greasing the wheels indefinitely. You will never be able to quit. They know it. I know it. Now you know it, too. It doesn't matter what the product is, in MLM there's no serious income to be made from merely selling the product. You must always be looking for someone else to sell the product, who will be on the prowl for someone else to sell the product, and so on down the line.

Can a fisherman throw out his lines and leave them unattended? Cast out his net and never gather it in again? Neither can the upline manager, director, distributor, or consultant. To be and stay *upline* means you will have to build and constantly rebuild your *downline*—forever. Why? Because of the incredible turnover that is a fact in MLM. People realize they aren't making money, so they quit. You have to keep replacing the ones who leave with new ones who don't know any better. It's a vicious cycle that never ends.

With all three MLMs I've been successfully involved in, I found that the allure of residual income is a lie. Every time people started making big money, the company I worked for changed the compensation plan to make it more difficult for people to keep earning those paychecks. One time it happened right before Christmas. We all got our paychecks, and they were down by 50 percent. The home office had been telling us that the compensation plan was going to change, but it would hurt only those who weren't really working the business. The truth was, it hurt everyone.

ALLURE: Walk the beaches of Hawaii with the spouse and kids someday.

HOOK: Until then, business will always come before family. You'll sacrifice time you will never get back and family who may never return to the closeness you have or used to have. By the time you get to Maui, you may not have a family left. You can't replace lost years with money.

In 1993, I took my family on a week-long cruise to the Caribbean. While everyone looking on thought it was pretty exciting and spectacular, my children were backslidden and bitter for being neglected for so many years. My marriage was so strained from my being married to MLM that Chuck and I hardly talked during the cruise. There were actually times when all the family did was bicker and fight.

ALLURE: Make all the money you want and still have plenty to do great things for God.

HOOK: If you want to sell the dream to others, you will be required to increase your standard of living to promote it. That's how you continually build your downline business. You will need even more money to feed the standard of living sandtrap. Altruistic at first, it is rare that the percentage of giving increases proportionate to income. Neither will you have time to spend in ministry yourself!

With one company I made over $100,000 a year and never gave more than 10 percent of my income. Why? I had built such a high overhead to look successful that I never had discretionary income with which to give and help others. Even when I made over $20,000 a month with another company, I found many other things to do with the money. My percentage of giving never increased with my income.

ALLURE: You can make a six-figure income.
HOOK: You will sell your soul and try to buy the souls of all your friends to do it. But the truth is that only 1 percent ever make over $50,000. Count them: That's five figures, not six.

Yes, I was one of the few who did make that six-figure income. But putting my experience up on a pedestal hooked thousands of others to go for it. They risked everything to reach for that golden ring. In every company I was in, less than 1 percent made big money. Those who did were exalted to cause others to covet what they had, even though the odds were never in their favor.

ALLURE: MLM is *the* answer to all your problems and money woes. MLM is the wave of the future.
HOOK: Once you nibble at this alluring bait, watch out. MLM has a set of problems all its own. Even if your family is still speaking to you, your friends will start avoiding you.

In MLM I found myself viewing anyone who wasn't involved as a loser. Society was lost because it hadn't accepted MLM. I was sure I was right and everyone else was wrong. The scripture "Pride cometh before a fall" (Prov. 16:18) never registered on my hardened heart. The hook that convinced me that I had, in fact, found the answer was lodged in my heart.

ALLURE: MLM is completely without risk. Once you pay your dues for the first few years, your residual income will be like getting something for nothing.

HOOK: Your life hangs on this hook. The dangers and risks are incredible. Many people have found themselves without friends, family, and even spouses when their MLM was shut down because of compromise and illegal practices. For those involved in legitimate MLMs, many made it to the next level only to discover they came alone. Their wife or husband left the marriage.

MLM comes with great risk. I risked the relationship with my husband and my children and almost lost them. When I decided that I was right and my husband was wrong about this MLM dream, I stepped out from under his spiritual authority and protection. I was fair game for the enemy of my soul to deceive me to an even greater level, and that is exactly what he did. At one point I was willing to choose my MLM over my marriage and children. Thank the Lord that He had mercy on me so I could come to my senses before doing something irrevocably stupid.

ALLURE: Everyone who signs on can be a winner.

HOOK: Like every gamble, winners only win at the expense of the losers. In many cases those are the people living in your house or going to your church. No money is created in MLM. The money you and your friends put into it is merely redistributed. It doesn't take intelligent people long to discover that if they sign on with you, their money will soon find its way into your account and into that of your upline. Unless, of course, they build a downline of their own.

The truth is the winners are very dependent on an unlimited supply of losers. Don't buy into the misconception that everybody can make more money than they invest. It's mathematically impossible. Ever wonder how some distributors will receive big bonus checks, larger than their investment? Because most distributors will receive smaller or no bonus checks at all. Think of it like a lottery: You don't buy a lottery ticket on the premise that you might win but that countless thousands of others will lose. How long would the lottery concerns be in business if they promised everyone would be a winner? No MLM can pay out more than it takes in, especially with overhead, bonuses, advertising, training, and recruiting expenses. This is the absolute truth: MLM leaders make money because somebody at the bottom is losing. Redistributing the wealth is far different than creating it.

I can remember putting on opportunity meetings and telling people in the audience that every single one of them had the God-given right to succeed in MLM. I was so sincere. I had come to believe that the only reason people did't make it in MLM is because of their bad attitude, their "stinkin' thinkin'." I never wanted to look at the mathematical facts that prove the impossibility of everyone being able to succeed!

Pam wrote me these comments:

> After attending a few meetings, my husband became convinced MLM was the way for us to reach our financial dreams. He signed up. What neither he nor I realized was that very day I became an MLM widow; our son, an MLM orphan. It was as if this new way of life invaded our entire home, schedule, and relationship. He didn't need us anymore; he had them. His upline became his parents, his downline his children. He left us home while he attended motivational seminars, training retreats, and weekend rallies. He brought in printed literature, books, and tapes that promoted a workaholic lifestyle and total dedication to his business. Loyalty and prosperity were the doctrines of his new belief. He was slipping from my grasp, and I could do nothing to stop it. We were losing touch.
>
> It didn't seem to matter to him. He was still in touch with his voice-mail each day and notes on the fax machine and eventually e-mail.
>
> In one year, he invested nearly $20,000 in tapes, books, and other motivational material and upline-sponsored events. His inventory investment, granted, was small. But by the time we computed our income tax, we discovered that he had earned only twenty dollars. That's right, *twenty dollars.*

In one year we were financially ruined. The remodeling project was never finished. Unfortunately, our marriage was.

How did this happen? Because Pam and her husband were looking for something that was looking for them—MLM. Pam's husband responded to the approach, was drawn in by the allure, and swallowed the hook. He was caught.

I started this chapter with a letter from Nan. How do you think Pam would respond to Nan's query? This book is the only way I know to get the many Pams and multiple Nans together.

Then I would say to all the people who identify with Nan's experience: "MLM companies may promise fellowship, fulfillment, independence, and wealth. But very few, if any, deliver on that promise. It's all an illusion—appealing allure—and it comes with a hook. In other words, all that glitters is certainly *not* God."

In His most loving way, God warns us when He says:

I know that after I leave, savage wolves will come in among you and will not spare the flock. Even from your own number men will arise and distort the truth in order to draw away disciples after them. (Acts 20:29–30)

We all have seen the helpless fish, squirming and thrashing about in the water at the end of the line, hook firmly snagged in its wide-open mouth. Once in a while they get away. Occasionally they are thrown back. It is possible to get out at this level, before stooping to the next level of MLM involvement. Not easy, mind you. But you can still get free, even if you've bitten on the allure and swallowed the hook.

1. *Admit there is a possibility you are being baited.* Learn to be biblically skeptical. The Bible says, "There is a way that seems right to a man, but in the end it leads to death" (Prov. 14:12). You might have to admit that you made an error in judgment in getting into MLM even this far. Ask God to protect you from any way that *seems* right but isn't.

2. *Pray for discernment.* The voices coming at you at this point are slick, rehearsed, and professionally practiced. Take some time to step aside and have a spiritual hearing check. How well have you heard God's voice before? Read some good books on hearing His voice. My favorite is *Hearing God* by Peter Lord. Remember, the Bible says, "The sheep listen to his voice. He calls his own sheep by name and leads them out" (John 10:3*b*).

3. *Let God examine your heart.* Ask Him to show you what He finds there. This is the time to be fully open with God. Yes, you may find some unpleasant or ugly things there, but swallow your pride. You can't afford to make a mistake as costly as being in disobedience to the Holy Spirit's voice and God's will for your life. Use the Psalmist's prayer of Psalm 139:23–24: "Search me, O God, and know my heart; test me and know my anxious thoughts. See if there is any offensive way in me, and lead me in the way everlasting."

4. *Ask God to make you willing to let go of the dream.* Surrender your will completely to Jesus Christ and then ask God for the strength and courage it will take to turn away from those things that would sink their hook deep within your soul and mind. Say a committed prayer like this one, "Create in me a pure heart, O God, and renew a steadfast spirit within me" (Ps. 51:10).

5. *Don't depend on how you feel or what you want.* You have listened to too much propaganda specifically prepared and aimed at your heart. You have to rely on the Word of God now. "The heart is deceitful above all things and beyond cure. Who can understand it? I the LORD search the heart and examine the mind, to reward a man according to his conduct, according to what his deeds deserve" (Jer. 17:9–10).

   Write down everything that attracted you to MLM, then hold them up to God for examination. Do they measure up against His Word? Is there even a slight chance you are being deceived?

6. *Repent.* If you realize that you have listened to the lusts of the flesh and let materialism draw your attention away from God's voice, you need to repent. Turn away now before you get in any deeper. Ask God to forgive you for letting your heart be drawn away from anything that is not of Him or from Him. Remember the promise of the Bible, "If we confess our sins, he is faithful and just and will forgive us our sins and purify us from all unrighteousness" (1 John 1:9).

7. *Ask God to show you why you are drawn away to the dreams and fantasies of MLM.* Are there some areas in your heart that need healing? Has there been abuse in your background that is still unresolved? Is there any unforgiveness lurking that drives you to "show 'em" and take reckless risks to prove yourself? Let God heal you. "He heals the brokenhearted and binds up their wounds" (Ps. 147:3). Have you let God love you in this healing way?

8. *Ask God to give you discernment and godly wisdom.* Be determined to be done with double-mindedness and to remain single in heart and purpose—God's purpose. "If any of you lacks wisdom, he should ask God, who gives generously to all without finding fault, and it will be given to him. But when he asks, he must believe and not doubt, because he who doubts is like a wave of the sea, blown and tossed by the wind. That man should not think he will receive anything from the Lord; he is a doubleminded man, unstable in all he does" (James 1:5–8).

9. *Ask God to show you what He wants for your life.* Ask Him how He wants to use the gifts, talents, and time He has given you. Ask Him where you fit into the kingdom. "Commit to the LORD whatever you do, and your plans will succeed" (Prov. 16:3).

10. *Tell God you're willing to give it all up.* Then have the courage to walk away. Say no even if it means you will lose the friendship of the one who is trying to recruit you or the one who succeeded. Your life is "hidden with Christ in God" (Col. 3:3). God has great plans for your life. Let these words

be your strength and personal mission statement: "For *I am* God's workmanship, created in Christ Jesus to do good works, which God prepared in advance for *me* to do" (Eph. 2:10, paraphrased).

This is the time to surrender your will, your agenda, your desires, your wants, your business, and your future to Jesus. Go away for a weekend somewhere out in nature. The goal is to get some solitude. Don't take your pager, your cell phone, your Daytimer, your goal sheets. Just take your Bible, a journal to write in, and some juice. Fast for the entire time and commit to seeking the Lord's face in this matter. Pray earnestly that you will hear His voice above all others.

Surrender, surrender, surrender.

Yield to the work of the Holy Spirit in you. Ask Him to show you the truth. Ask Him to give you eyes to see and ears to hear what the Spirit of the Lord is saying in regard to your involvement in MLM. Be willing to ask God to help you not to make a mistake or commit an error in judgment. Tell the Lord that you're not leaving until you know what He wants you to do or not do on the issue. Ask Him to strip all unhealthy beliefs and justifications away from you and to replace them with the truths in His Word.

But if you're beyond this?

Perhaps you have already swallowed the hook and feel like you're in too deep to just say no. It's not too late. You can still break free of the sweet deceit of multi-level marketing. I did, and I was in much, much deeper than that.

4

Swallowing the Sweet Deceit

So where along the way into setting up your new small business venture does it happen? Exactly when does the desire for a little extra cash and financial security turn into cash mania? When does the strategy to give you more time for the family, more time and money for the things of God, give way to an obsession for amassing money? How does this happen and why?

It happens because of a well-designed plan to sell you on a dream that is based on a mathematical impossibility for success. At the same time, it connects with a person's insatiable drive to do and be more. It happens because as Christians we haven't learned the secret of contentment. It's what our friends at the Minirth-Meier Clinic refer to as *drivenness*—the epidemic of our day.[3]

Sweet deceit comes in the form of a plan hiding a subtle switch. The switch is simply this: "We don't really want you to sell our products. We want you to sell the idea of other people selling our products." And of course we want you to sell them on the idea of finding other people to sell our products that you can actually sell on the idea of finding still more people to . . . Ad infinitum. For the Christian, this is where the parallel to Jesus and the Twelve Apostles comes into play and is used and abused to rationalize the MLM downline philosophy. Without really noticing, the training and motivation meetings no longer push the products; they push the idea of wealth and the dream of financial independence. The entire emphasis, though expertly hidden in cleverly prepared audio-visual presentations, is now on recruitment. Building your own personal downline, or as some say, helping others help themselves.

So, how did you get from "How would you like to make a few extra dollars each month?" to an emphasis on personal wealth? How did it get so far so fast? In my first MLM experience I would hear things presented from the stage like, "There are only so many hours in a day. You can only do so much. You can only sell so much. The only way to multiply your efforts and be a good steward of the time God has given you is to build an organization of people who will go out there and sell, whether you get out there or not." This made so much sense to me at the time. As a result, I never questioned the ethical standards I would have to ignore in order to begin seeing people as a means to an end.

THE MLM MARCH TO A MILLION

It began way back at what I have called the *approach,* progressed one more step when you flirted with the *allure.* And buried deep within that appealing allure was the *hook*—the dream of making it big. Earn a little extra each month? Why settle for so little when you have the chance to forget your financial woes and grab your piece of the American Dream? Once you swallow the allure, the hook is set. And here you are, squarely facing the sweet deceit.

If you doubt that it is true, listen carefully to the presentation at your next opportunity meeting. See if you can identify the change in emphasis:

- From faith in the product to faith in prosperity
- From the reality of the product to the rationalization of the dream-like appeal
- From the merits of the product to the peddling of the health/wealth doctrine (available only through your product, of course)
- From being the bridge between manufacturer and consumer marketplace to being the targeted market for motivational hype—tapes, books, and printed literature keeping the faith pumped in imminent prosperity

Is it not somewhat like the snake-oil peddler convincing his audience of an illness, then selling them the cure? When I was busy building my downline, that was my strategy: Find a person's hot button and push it! Find out what frustrates her about her job and explain how MLM is the opposite of that frustration.

At one point in my involvement in selling a diet product, the company began to shift its focus onto nutrition rather than dieting. This was due to pressure from the Food and Drug Administration. It was at that time that we started reading different MLM books and realized that there were way more people interested in making extra money than there were people interested in good health. That's when we began to change our focus in the meetings and presentations to be geared around making money rather than getting healthy. Thus, the transition from product to opportunity. The MLM distribution system convinces recruits of their discontent, uncertain futures, and go-nowhere lives, then sells them the cure: the MLM motivational material found in the training tapes, books, rallies, and opportunities.

In the largest MLM company in existence, selling inspirational tapes to downline sales reps is a more profitable business to MLM's largest distributors than selling the products themselves. Officially they may be treated as sales tools, but in many organizations the inspirational and motivational material containing the official MLM doctrine of dreams has risen beyond the status of marketing material to that of official product.[4]

While the MLM you are considering has approached you to sell soap, fingernail polish, vitamins, or long-distance service, what they are selling has nothing to do with any of those things. It has to do with *you*. Authors Robert Fitzpatrick and Joyce K. Reynolds wrote the following in their book, *False Profits:* "They want to sell you a new faith. Not one that is founded on biblical principles of sacrifice and *giving,* but faith in prosperity—the doctrine of *getting*—without any of the social or biblical consequences. In other words, they want you to buy into a movement that enrolls thousands of new recruits in the face of 99 percent economic casualty rates."[5] One in a hundred succeed. Ninety-nine fail.

If you invest only one hundred dollars, you can shrug it off, count yourself lucky, and get back on track, smarter and less gullible. But what if you are one of the people who have invested $1,500 or even more to be able to sell distributorships? I don't know about you, but when I swallowed the hook I also swallowed the pitch of the switch—all in one huge gulp! I justified it all with big and glorious plans for the money I could earn. I wasn't going to spend all that MLM prize money on foolish things, like flashy cars and fancy clothes. Not me. I had my feet on the ground. I would use the money to help support my husband's ministry. I would give generously to the church's building fund. When the money really started rolling in, I'd funnel it right back out to missions and world evangelism. Right?

Hand in hand, denial and greed worked their magic on me just as they had on Greg. Ideas of moving up to a nicer house with a view; trading in my car for a newer, more expensive model; taking the family on a cruise; buying a new wardrobe; and having extra spending money began to crowd out the godly things I planned for the money.

And the Word of God? Nothing could have been further from my mind.

Do not love the world or the things in the world. If anyone loves the world, the love of the Father is not in him. For all that is in the world—the lust of the flesh, the lust of the eyes, and the pride of life—is not of the Father but is of the world. (1 John 2:15–16 NKJV)

The sweet deceit of MLM had brought me to the same place as countless numbers of other sincere Christians who have bought into its lies and allure. It took me many years, many attempts, and many programs and products before I realized that I wasn't a marketer. I was the *market.* Just like thousands of others, I couldn't see it. I was too blinded by the lust of my own flesh, the lust of my own eyes, and the pride of having my own life. If you had said that a dedicated Christian like me was actually checking out of the plan of the Father's kingdom and buying into the world's system of lust and greed, you would have heard me protest very loudly indeed. (That is, if you could actually get me to listen as I brushed by you, hurrying on my way to another motivational meeting or MLM pep rally.) After all, I believed in what I was doing. I believed that it was not only right but blessed by God. Infused with such misbelief, I was totally intolerant of any whom would dare to give me a word of caution. Negative thinkers didn't belong—not in my downline, certainly not in my circle of friends.

And where was all this amassing of wealth leading me? I had no idea. But no matter, I was far too busy to be concerned or to listen to those who were—including Chuck, my husband. Those who didn't see the MLM dream as I did simply had not caught on or weren't capable of visionary thinking. How was I to know that the success of my upline actually depended on the failure of my downline?

Shocking? It's true.

The MLM false doctrine in its very nature is based on the hopes and the failures of those on the bottom of the line. Success for any MLM is based on recruiting—the selling of family and friends for profit. If too many succeed, the MLM structure collapses or they change the compensation plan to make it harder to earn income on your downline. The sheer weight of countless MLMers all selling and recruiting would quickly consume entire markets. There would be no more customers left, no more people to recruit. Do the numbers yourself.

If one person recruited five people, who in turn recruited five more, each who in turn . . . Within a very short time, just nine steps of recruitment, 9,765,625 would be involved. Think of it this way:

5
25
125
625
3,125
15,625
78,125
390,625
1,953,125
9,765,625

And what would you have to do to recruit the entire population of Los Angeles and neighboring cities? Recruit five, who would recruit five, who would recruit more. What was that we were selling? Pills, water filters, cosmetics, soap? Would your favorite product even have ten million customers in your town, let alone distributors? Mine wouldn't. That's for sure.

You might be saying, "I won't recruit distributors. I'll just recruit salespeople." Go ahead, tell your upline about your wonderful plan. Their reaction will probably let you know whether you are really in the product business or not.

And if we're no longer in the product business, what business are we in?

Oh, you'll get *something* for your modest start-up investment. You may be able to get tax write-offs. Maybe even a year or two of losses. You will certainly be able to get the product at a discount, some of which you might actually like and use. When you're down and discouraged, you'll get to attend the motivational meetings and get another stiff dose of the dream. Maybe you'll even make a few bucks here and there.

You'll certainly get to meet new friends. After alienating most of your old ones, you probably could use a few new ones. But remember, *using* your old ones is how you got here. And family? MLM can replace those who are tired of listening to the empty promises and don't believe the dangling carrot is real anymore. MLM will be your family now. Just look at your upline as your parents and your downline as your children. You'll also probably end up with a garage full of product, more than you can sell or use. How will you justify your miniwarehouse? Don't worry, you'll learn how to sidestep the hard questions posed by your husband or wife.

Remember, you can't tell anyone how difficult this really is. You never know when you might be talking to a potential recruit. Think positive. That will have to be your motto now. You can't tell anyone how you're really doing. Anyone who asks will have to get the standard rehearsed answer, "Great! Business is wonderful." After all, you've never seen anything grow so fast or bring in the extra income so quickly and so easy. Right? Of course, that is, if you still believe the sweet deceit of MLM. After all, you've decided to go with the flow, which is really the sweetest deceit of all—the money flow.

Where Did All That Money Flow?

In a usual business a man or woman has a great idea for a product. He either sells the idea or invests his own money to become the manufacturer himself. Then the manufacturer builds the great product and seeks the best and most efficient way to get the great product to the end user, the consumer. It is sold either wholesale or retail, and the customers pay the manufacturer. The manufacturer deposits the money and writes out employee paychecks and sales commissions. The money flow falls like gentle water, rippling naturally down through the woods toward the valley below. Not so in MLM.

In MLM the money starts at the bottom and flows up. Defying the pull of even economic gravity, the distributor pays for the right to sell, rather than the salesman being paid from the sale. That's very good for the people at the top. Not so good for those at the bottom.

Why do we do it? Why did I? It's called *deception*. Like it or not, we fell for it—approach, allure, hook, and all. I fell for the switch, and then I wanted more. Sadly many of us got more than we wanted.

We wanted opportunity. What we got was a new philosophy. We wanted a part-time income for a few hours of work each week. What most of us got was very little income compared to our investment—and we worked a lot more than just a few hours a week! We thought this was an open door to buy the product wholesale, just for personal use, and perhaps for a few interested friends. What we got was a one-way door into the wild world of contests or new programs we had to be involved in just to keep our discounted percentage or ability to earn a little commission on the downline.

We thought we were getting into an opportunity to help our friends and other people. I don't know about you, but I ended up enslaving others and causing others to stumble into the same trap that had ensnared me. I thought MLM would give me control over my own schedule. I discovered that my MLM business ended up controlling me and determining my schedule. The phone never stopped ringing at all hours of the day and night, and people were always stopping by. I dreamed of having money for ministry and other benevolent causes, but there certainly wasn't any money left for God once I cranked up the successful image treadmill to full speed.

I bought into the idea of working from home but soon found MLM had invaded and conquered my home. The very dream that had promised me more time with my family and husband intruded on the innermost areas of our lives. There was no place to escape. The business sapped all my energy and free time so I didn't nurture those who were supposed to mean the most to me. I believed the sacrifice was worth the future payoff. How wrong I was! MLM was supposed to give me more time with loved ones. But that day never came. I kept putting my family on hold—just until the business was on its own two feet.

Even though I worked from home, I was always on the phone. "Can't talk to Mom right now. Sorry, kids. Later." The telephone was always perched on my shoulder and my personal organizer was always within reach. My downline actually came before my own husband and family. I was so blind to it; I couldn't even see the pain I caused Chuck and the kids. It wasn't until after my moment of truth that I could actually see the devastation I had caused by my wrong choices and unhealthy behavior.

Deeper into the sweet deceit I longed for world travel, long exotic vacations with the family I had shoved aside to make enough money to give them the vacation. But when I was actually strolling a distant tropical beach and lounging on the deck of a cruise ship, I found myself with an estranged husband and bitter, backslidden children.

I also believed the lie that MLM was the pathway to security. In the process I almost lost my emotional security. I dreamed and longed for financial independence, but all I realized was personal debt to keep the business going. I reasoned, *I just have to work harder, that's all. The rainbow ends just past the next level or with the next ground-floor opportunity, then the pot of gold will be mine, all mine!* I dug myself in deeper and deeper, all the while believing in my own self-reliance and boundless energy to pull it off. Chuck and the kids would have to wait just a bit more. Eventually they'd come around. One day they'd look back and see that the sacrifices had been worth it—*wouldn't they?*

I had been depending on my MLM dream the way we're supposed to depend on God. MLM had become my Jehovah-Jireh, my provider. In other words, while the sweet deceit of MLM had promised me the dream of freedom, the reality was a nightmare of captivity.

So How Do We Get Out at This Point?

I'm sure you've heard the expression, "Run—do not walk—to the nearest exit." But even more practical than that, listen to the words of 1 Timothy 6:6–11:

> But godliness with contentment is great gain. For we brought nothing into the world, and we can take nothing out of it. But if we have food and clothing, we will be content with that. People who want to get rich fall into temptation and a trap and into many foolish and harmful desires that plunge men into ruin and destruction. For the love of money is a root of all kinds of evil. Some people, eager for money, have wandered from the faith and pierced themselves with many griefs. But you, man of God, flee from all this, and pursue righteousness, godliness, faith, love, endurance, and gentleness.

Flee! Run! Get out of there!

Look at this list of tips:

1. Critically explore whether or not the plan or program you are involved in offers commissions to recruit new members. Be aware that this could also happen as part of the compensation plan, where larger discounts are available when you have a certain size downline or where significant money is offered only in connection with recruiting others.

   If so, this will only indoctrinate you into viewing people as potential recruits rather than someone who needs the Lord. It will also move you into a realm where you focus on getting something for nothing by finding good people who will go out and build a big downline that will earn you commissions. *Run, and run fast!*

   On the other hand, how about you? How were you recruited? Have you finally learned to be cautious? Beware of over-friendly people. If they are friendly to you with no obvious reason, chances are they want something from you—and it probably includes your pocketbook, friends, and family.

2. Are you being asked to spend money on inventory? In one MLM I was involved in, we encouraged people to charge the $3,000–$5,000 in inventory so they could go direct to the top. This practice taught Christians to bypass the Lord and take things into their own hands by using credit. I have reduced my philosophy about this to one simple statement: If you have to charge it, you're already operating in the flesh!

3. Does your company claim that you will make more money by recruiting instead of selling product yourself? If so, you will forever be looking for people to buy your program. This will destroy your friendships and family relationships. It will also cause you to sum up a person's value based on his or her ability to benefit your business. Is it any wonder such shallow, commercialized relationships go sour?

   Don't try to justify that you're only going to sell the product. When others like the product, you'll have to tell them that they can sign up and get it for wholesale. That will expose them to the company mentality of building a downline for fame and fortune, allowing them to be enticed by the possibility of worldly possessions and financial independence. Once they are a distributor, they are in the company's database and will receive all the company propaganda whether you like it or not. It's exploitation— you were exploited, you exploited, and those you have exploited will exploit. *Run—run fast!*

4. Are there exaggerated promises about high profits or claims about miracle products? Remember, if it sounds too good to be true, it probably is. These kinds of promises tend to draw us away from God's promises and the miracle-working power of the Holy Spirit and into man-made promises and products.

   Are the performance claims provable and from *reliable* sources, or are they simply believable testimonials?

Well-intentioned people giving scripted testimonials can be very convincing. Especially when all the thanks and glory is given to God. Some of those very product claims and testimonials have been brought into court and disproved.

Sometimes we do see companies with outstanding products. Furthermore, because the product is so good and performs well, this opens the door to the person being recruited. It's funny, but we just seem to assume that if the product is great, God *must* want us to sell it. Why is that? How do we make such presumptions? Like I've said over and over, just because the door is open does not mean God wants us to go through it!

5. Have you been asked for a list of family or friends? If so, *run—run fast*. You are going to exploit your personal relationships for personal gain. This will not only destroy many of your relationships but will defile those you approach in this manner. Don't buy the lie that you are doing them a favor. This is just a way for you to rationalize the guilt you feel for using the relationship so you can get something you want. Doing so will only quench the Holy Spirit, Who is trying to keep you from defiling those you love.

6. Have you been asked to pay money or sign up in a high-pressure situation? Most MLM meetings suggest that waiting is a sign of laziness, stupidity, and lack of finesse and true business savvy. You might be told that, if you wait, someone else might sign up your friend or family member, and then you'll lose out on all those commissions. This kind of pressure is manipulation and nothing short of witchcraft. If the Lord really wants you to be involved, He'll make it clear after much prayer. Wait and let Him confirm it, and you won't have to worry about losing out or not getting in on the ground floor.

7. Have you checked out the company with the Better Business Bureau or even the state attorney general's office? If not, do your homework! You'll be surprised at what you find. Then . . . *run—run fast!*

One thing I've noticed in MLM, each organization considers itself elite. Without a second thought, they slander other MLMs, saying they have the best compensation plan, best perks, best product, best leadership, and on and on. This mentality is more than just cutthroat competition; it is cultlike in nature and sets people up to isolate in their system—viewing all other companies as less than theirs. The spirit of competition is alive and well in MLM. That opens the door to the spirit of gossip and slander, and it filters into the downline!

I have never seen such rampant gossip as I have seen in MLM, especially among those who have been involved for many years and/or have gone from one company to another. One woman I would consider to be an MLM junkie (and a professing Christian at that) used to call me and gossip about the leadership. She talked about the founder of the company and the home office. Many of her comments were wild tales that would cause most people to fly into a state of panic. All along, she was simply setting up her excuses to exit and go to another company, hoping to take me and my downline with her. I didn't fall for it, but I know many others who did.

8. Is your spouse wholeheartedly in agreement? If not, this is one of the ways that God holds us accountable and tries to keep us from making disastrous mistakes. If we do not heed the caution of our spouse, we are setting ourselves up for certain disaster. If in doubt, look for the way out and *run— run fast!* So many times Chuck saw me slipping away from him, from the kids, and from the Lord. He tried so hard to talk sense into me, but I was unteachable, unyielding, not submitted. I was so sure I was right. Oh, if I'd only used his response as a test as to whether God was really in it, I would have saved myself so much heartache!

How do you guard your heart against the sweet deceit of MLM, with all its dreams of millions of dollars and materialism? Call it what it is: greed. Then stay away. Choose contentment instead. Honor God in your friendships; honor God in your family relationships; honor God in your money; and honor God with your time. Learn, like the apostle Paul, the secret of living way above the American Dream—in contentment. You want to chase something? Follow his advice to Timothy, a young man about to embark on life and ministry. "But you, man of God, flee from all this, and pursue righteousness, godliness, faith, love, endurance, and gentleness" (1 Tim. 6:11).

That pursuit is worth the effort.

5

Hooked: The Addiction of MLM

"I would have to admit," Janet said, "that only a year ago, I would have laughed at the idea of getting involved with network marketing. After all, I had my experiences, just as almost everyone else has. I must say, I walked away from most of these encounters with less than a favorable impression of network marketing. It all seemed so underhanded, almost dishonest, and expensive.

"And yet here I am now, smack dab in the middle of a marketing trend that is unquestionably going to change the way we live our lives as we enter the twenty-first century. The more I have learned and listened about network marketing over the past year, the more excited and confident I have become that it is an industry in transition from the covert traps and scam operations of the '80s to a legitimate and widely respected means of doing business in the '90s and beyond. I'm sold on this cutting-edge business. I'm excited to share my products with my family and friends and not only that—but to offer them the same moneymaking opportunity as I have! After all, this is about friends helping friends. It's all about networking with my family, friends, and other acquaintances. I'm not doing a really big business yet, but I've only been at it a year. By this time next year . . ."

But does Janet actually know what she's gotten into? Do you?

You've been to at least one presentation or recruitment meeting. It may not have made sense before, but something has finally clicked. Suddenly it sounds exciting and fun. You've met people who have confided that they are making more than $10,000 each month. Even if you just worked part time, you'd be thrilled with one-third that amount. The allure is too strong. You've got your pen poised over the checkbook ready to make the investment in yourself, in your dreams, in your future. But wait. *Stop!*

There is another side to the story—a side you can't afford *not* to hear. Unless you've been there, it's hard to believe. But I've been there; I know firsthand. The dream of "making it" fuels any unhealthy addictive behavior many of us have lurking just beneath the surface. Once hooked, it's like any other addiction, whether gambling, drugs, or even pornography. Once hooked, even a fresh revelation from the Word of God or just spending time in His majestic presence pales in comparison.

"My son has gotten into multi-level marketing," a worried mother writes. "It scares me. He's like a religious fanatic or someone in a cult. He doesn't want to hear anything negative about how he's changed or how much he's let this thing take over his life. I've tried to talk to him," she said. "But he just told me he'd been taught how to deal with negative people, and that I was one of the negative people. He's a young man, too immature to see trouble coming down the road. He thinks he's found the answer to success. I think he's getting in over his head, but he won't listen. He tries to recruit all his friends. It's got so that nobody wants to be around him anymore. So now he's out all the time just going places to meet new friends. Unfortunately, he has only one thing on his mind: how to get people to sign up under him."

It's hard to resist when you've been promised the most incredible moneymaking and profit-generating strategic financial program ever. Who doesn't want to believe there is an actual program in which nobody ever loses—a way that everybody wins? The dream is like a carrot dangling in front of you. You get addicted to the chase, to the competition, to the excitement of getting to that next level. You get to the point where life is boring and not meaningful if there isn't the rush of adrenaline and hype. You live for the next contest, a new bonus, a new product. You long for a new strategy to talk about with your downline. And the saddest part of all, for many it's only an illusion. It's like chasing bubbles with a butterfly net.

I'll never forget the time I made the big push for a promotion to senior vice president. I was always coming up with a contest to keep the sales coming in, and this particular month I had two contests going at the same time to really get things moving. One contest was a steak and beans contest. My downline was split into two teams. The losing team not only had to eat cold beans out of a can, but they had to serve the winners their steak on china and exquisite linen tablecloths. Then I offered to pay an extra fifty dollars out of my own earnings for every sale made during my qualifying month. I knew it would be worth it because of the significant increase in bonuses I would receive as a senior vice president. The two contests and my unrelenting drive helped me make that big promotion. But wouldn't you know it, the very next month the company discontinued the bonus payout to senior vice presidents!

Ken and Marianne York wanted to believe in the MLM success dream. They tried to believe it for seven long months. "Never made a dime," Ken said. "But nobody can say I didn't try. I spent over $3,000 trying as hard as I knew how. I went to the conventions; I bought the inventory; I attended the motivational meetings."

"They say you don't have to sell anything," Marianne offered. "They told us once our friends and family found out we were in a new business, they'd want to buy our products and even join under us to help us out. That's not what happened at all."

"It became a full-time job," Ken said. "That's not at all what I wanted. This was supposed to be supplemental income. You know, something Marianne and I could do together, and she'd be able to stay home with the kids. I tried to recruit, but it just didn't work. And then I started noticing that the people I met at the conventions didn't seem to be doing all that well either. Some of them really appeared to be quite desperate. I got out, took the loss off my taxes, and counted myself one of the lucky ones."

He's more right than he even realizes.

Bill wrote this letter to me:

I have been caught up in several MLM groups. Since I am a manic depressive, I work like a madman during the manic phases then crash and burn during the depressive times. MLM fuels this problem more than any other thing in my whole life. Thank God for your book. . . . I got out of MLM, and with God's help I now consider myself 'MLM-proof.' I can't tell you how wonderful it is to have my life back again. It's great to greet my friends now with no hidden agendas.

When Downline Dreams Turn into Nightmares

Is MLM really that addictive? Linda thinks so.

My husband got hooked into MLM about six years ago. He believed a famous Christian TV personality and bought it all. It didn't take very long, and he was looking at everyone he knew or even met as prospects—certainly not as individuals with needs or even souls. Soon our friends didn't want to talk to us anymore. Within a short time we sold our house and leased a huge house to hold his recruiting and downline meetings in. But it never did get off the ground. Eventually we lost the house, and after other tries at MLM we lost another $50,000. Finally the light went off in my head but not his. I'm sorry to say it all led to our divorce, leaving our family damaged and broken. The sad thing is, he is still hooked. He's still waiting for his ship to come in. He can't see he's missed the biggest and best boat of all; our marriage and family was on it and left without him.

Tragically Linda's story isn't all that unusual. People get hooked on the dreams and promises of MLM each and every day. Hopefully you won't be one of those who are so addicted to the excitement of MLM that you're far too busy to confront the difficult issues in life—the hurts and wounds that may be behind your workaholism. I remember what that's like. The busier I was, the more addicted I became and the easier it was to stuff my wounds and emotional needs and not have to deal with them. Eventually I came to my moment of truth, and if you're hooked on MLM, your moment of truth will come sooner or later.

Another woman wrote:

> I just read your article, "Escape from Greed," in *Charisma* magazine, and it defines everything I have been trying to tell my husband since he was lured into MLM. He lives and breathes this business—all the books, tapes, and functions and whatever else his upline tells him. At the sacrifice of almost everything we owned, and almost our marriage, he continues to struggle to make his business work.
>
> I have prayed that he would hear from God and see that this is not God's way to financial success. We have lost both cars and most of our furniture and have almost had to live on the street because of this. It has not occurred to him yet that this business is not a blessing from God. He is so consumed with the hopes and hype of MLM that we barely see each other anymore.
>
> What can I do? How can I reach him before it's too late?

DREAMSELLERS

"I'm interested in building a company on people's hopes and dreams," said Linden Wood of Excel Communications.

When you realize that the stated goals of many MLMs can be summed up in these few words, you begin to understand where the underlying power of MLM's allure really is. The gripping power of MLM is not in superior products. It's not in the basic premise of the friends-helping-friends concept of networking relationships. The real power of MLM is the promise of helping you realize your wildest financial dreams and richest hopes of being a success. No traditional job opportunity promises to make you a big shot, important and rich. What traditional corporation do you know that holds "motivationfests" for employees, pumping them up with promises that they can eventually equal the incomes and importance of its top executives? Their opportunities for advancement pale in comparison to the professionally produced audio-visual presentations of MLM companies that hold out fantasies of exotic vacations in a plush, faraway paradise.

Hooks, Lines, and Sinkers

We get hooked on MLM because we're hooked on our fantasies for bigger and better things. It's the promise that we can leave the world of cutthroat competition and "share" our way into happiness! We're hooked on anything that promises happiness. After all, isn't that the great American pursuit held out to each of us as a constitutional right? Isn't prosperity a right of every one of the King's kids? We get hooked on the dream of an easier way to do things. Hooked on the vision of being on the cutting edge—a pioneer worth noticing in the business world.

At a motivational convention Linden Wood proclaimed, "When I discovered Excel, I was still waiting for life to come to Linden. Well, that's the day I got an attitude and decided to meet destiny. We're here this weekend to get that attitude!"

"We'll call our company Amway," said Rich DeVos, one of the founders of the oldest and strongest MLM ever, "because the American way of private ownership and free enterprise is the best way."

Promises, Promises

There is nothing quite as addictive as a self-set attitude targeted toward the dream of taking control of one's own destiny and being a self-made millionaire. There's nothing quite as heady as setting yourself up as your own god. Uplines promise downlines that their hours will decrease as they become uplines in their own right and their downlines work to earn them money. There's nothing like the promise of the dream of one day being on top, instead of at the bottom, to get you hooked on MLM.

"This is my way out," one man said. "I need this opportunity. Something like this comes along only once in a lifetime—count me in."

Only once in a lifetime? Hardly. Since you have only one life, why would you want to embrace addictive-compulsive behavior and risk losing your family while you invest precious time and energy into making your upline wealthy? Is it the idea that one day you will convince someone else to subject himself or herself to the same compulsive addictions in order to make you wealthy? Does that sound like the plan God has for you?

Life Plus Everything Else

"I don't work it," Stan, a staunch MLMer said, "I live it! Everywhere I go I have my brochures, my business cards. While I get gas, the attendant hears about my business and how he could be in the business. I'm talking to my accountant and invite him in too. I visit with the courtesy clerk at my supermarket. I mention it to the waitress at the cafe. I show my brochures to the guys in my bowling league. I talk to other parents at my son's Little League game. I make it my goal to talk to at least two new people at my church fellowship functions. At my daughter's wedding I didn't pass up the opportunity to speak about the business to her new in-laws. It's what I do. I live it to the fullest. I help people, trust people, and build them up. Everyone knows this is the way business should be. It excites people to see me excited."

So, how many hours a week does this MLM addict actually work?

"How can you put a number on it? How many hours a week do I live? I live my work and work my life," Stan says with a big grin. You sense he has turned the MLM dream into a lifelong mission. Does he know he's hooked? "Completely," he says, "and proud of it."

Dreaming the Dream, Living the Nightmare

Does Stan's wife and family know he's hooked? Ask them how they feel when he sometimes spends more than he earns, on books, cassettes, videos, or conventions, trying to find the next big secret or feeding his motivational addiction. Stan's ego has become so enlarged that he finds it hard to associate with people who do not see what he sees, his wife included. Even she can't seem to wake him up from his fantasy world and MLM addiction.

The Blind Man Who Will Not See

Stan now buys product to better service his downline. "Speeds things up," he explains, "to have it all ready to go." His wife, however, is doubtful and hesitant to invest any more of their assets into the business. "Stinkin' thinkin'," Stan scolds when she voices her opinion. "You need a new attitude!"

Hooked, Lined, and Suckered

Our Western mentality of "more is better" is definitely fueled in MLM. Discontentment and dissatisfaction with the present is preached to motivate the troops to sell more, recruit more, and dream more. What's worse, this message never ends! Even when you make it big, someone is always bigger or has more. New motivation is created to move you toward building it bigger, getting to the next level, and making more money so you can make it even bigger.

Like willing junkies, we become addicted to the hype, to the warm fuzzies, to the effervescent relationships with our upline and downline people. Do we have the courage to admit that all those relationships are based on nothing more than the ulterior motive to get us to do more, recruit more, and make more sales so they can get more commissions off our sales? It doesn't matter. Junkies don't really care.

We convince ourselves that if we don't make it, it's must be our fault—certainly not the system. So we try again. We find another MLM; a newer, better compensation plan; a more miraculous product; a company where we can get in on the ground floor; and the addiction cycle escalates. We never admit to ourselves that there's something very wrong with the MLM system and that it just isn't good for us, period.

And why not? Because then we'd have to face the truth about MLM—the hype, the bogus dreams and fantastic wishes MLM pushes. And the truth sometimes hurts. No, we're not ready for the truth—at least not yet.

"Maybe later," the MLM junkie says, "after I've recruited everyone I know, ever have known, or ever will know. Until then I'll just continue going to the constant motivationfests, keep right on with the group-bonding activities with my up and downline people. I'll keep chasing after the dangling carrot of an obscenely excessive income. As long as I can see it, as long as I can almost taste it, touch it, and nearly hold it, I'll keep chasing that carrot—even if it's forever out of reach." That may sound silly, but it is what we say when we keep chasing the dream!

Unfortunately, there are those who will help keep the addiction alive. They're more than willing to feed the fixation and provide the pep talks that validate the MLM junkie's choice.

And why wouldn't they? After all, in one large MLM, feeding your addiction by pushing motivation conferences, tapes, books, and speeches makes them even wealthier than the products they are supposed to be selling.

Addiction, Plain and Simple

"Addictions have always been a part of the human predicament," say authors Dale and Juanita Ryan. "Addictions of one kind or another have always enslaved people. They have always led to spiritual, emotional, social, and sometimes physical death."[6] The Ryans define an addiction as "the habitual use of a substance or the habitual practice of a behavior to control one's mood in spite of the fact that the substance or the behavior creates repeated problems."

Drs. Hemfelt, Minirth, and Meier, in their book, *We Are Driven*, call drivenness ". . . the insatiable drive to do more and be more."

"Drivenness," the doctors explain, "often can lead to addictions—a word usually linked with drugs or alcohol." But they go on to say, "We believe people can be addicted to almost any kind of behavior or activity—work, fitness, perfectionism, sports, collecting antiques, rescuing other people, *acquiring financial status* . . ." (emphasis mine).[7]

"But," you protest, "I'm not addicted. At least not in the strictest sense of the word."

Oh, no?

Compulsivity is an addiction to achievement and accomplishment. Obsessive-compulsive behavior is based on the mistaken notion that mastery of my body, my performance, and my physical and material environment is the only true source of personal satisfaction and the only answer to my deepest emotional and spiritual hunger.[8]

Is This the Beginning of the End?

What would it take to make you snap? To push you over the edge? Only you can answer those questions. But do your answers have anything to do with your business? What if you were suddenly prevented from being involved with your MLM? What will you do when the mental strain and physical exhaustion overtake you? Drag yourself to another motivational meeting to get recharged? *To get your fix?*

I justified such behavior with the thoughts of how much good I just knew I would do with the money. After all, I hadn't bought into the dreams of fancy clothes, fine cars, and exotic vacations. Oh, how I fooled myself.

Did I underwrite the new building project like I promised myself I would? Did I really take on the support of more foreign missionaries? What do you think?

6 | How Does It Happen?

When vulnerability meets opportunity, watch out. Most of us struggle to make ends meet from time to time. Financial difficulties are not that rare. It's so easy to look at what we might consider hard times and ask, "When is it my turn, God? When do I get a break?"

It's not that unusual to let down our defenses when someone presents a solution to all our financial woes. When we're just managing to keep our heads above water, a friend in MLM encourages us to dream about being well-off. In the process, however, we often drop our guard.

I quickly lowered my guard at my first recruitment meeting. Once I was an MLM upline, I followed the same approach that worked with me. First I got people excited about the opportunity. That wasn't hard. After all, some of them had had little to get excited about for quite a while. They came wanting good news, and I gave them just what they wanted. I showed them graphically how bad their current situation was. I emphasized how their bills were either being paid late or not at all. I pounced on their lack of hope and magnified their fears. Then I began sowing seeds of discontent. Even if their jobs got better or they got a raise, could they match what I had to offer? Of course not.

Once I had painted a grim picture of their lives, I offered to rescue them from their terrible financial trap with my product and program. I eroded the credibility of corporate America by raising fear-based possibilities of mergers, takeovers, cutbacks, layoffs, transfers, demotions, and unfair evaluations. I also knew how to convincingly discredit small business and discourage owning any kind of franchise.

Once I had them convinced they had no freedom, no independence, and no joy, I raised fear for the future. I targeted retirement and blasted away at their security. I reminded them of important things in life: Give to the ministries of your choice, get your kids into Christian schools, double your tithe, spend more quality time with your family. Move into a nicer house, get a more reliable and comfortable car, and have more spendable cash every month. Finally I convinced them MLM is a way of life they could trust. I learned how to effectively and convincingly make them want what I offered and become discontent with what they had. The sad fact is I believed what I was telling them.

So how does it happen? Are they just weak and vulnerable people looking for easy answers? The Bible constantly reminds us how much we are all weak and in need of a Savior. There are times in everyone's life when we are vulnerable to fear and make wrong choices. We can be susceptible to the clever, subtle, powerful influences that have targeted our weakest point of vulnerability. It's not that unusual for intelligent, talented people to join MLM. It may look right and sound right, but it's wrong—sometimes deadly wrong.

We Forget Whose We Are

It is my opinion that MLM encourages self-centered, not God-centered, living. You and I have been bought with a price. When we accepted Christ as our Savior and gave God's will first place in our lives, we no longer had to be enslaved to sin; neither do we belong to ourselves any longer. Florence Bulle in *The Many Faces of Deception* put it this way:

> How times have changed! One thing I knew as a growing child: Christian discipleship was costly. One gave up the claim to success, fame, and wealth. A common song of commitment was "I Surrender All." Now I am told I can have the best of both worlds. The rags-to-riches prophets dangle the promise of material blessings as an enticement to follow Christ and prosperity as the birthright of all Christians.
>
> But are riches the lure that Jesus used when He called men and women to follow Him? Treasures in heaven—yes; treasures on earth—no.
>
> Jesus laid down some tough requirements for discipleship. To the man who said he would follow Jesus wherever He went, Jesus said nothing about profit. He talked about cost. Foxes have holes, and birds have nests, Jesus said, but He had no place to lay His head, no home on earth to call His own. Following Jesus meant a life in insecurity—if one needed material things in order to be secure.[9]

In our current possession- and image-driven culture, it is easy to forget that we've been called to live in the footprints of the Lamb. It's also easy to forget that the deceiver is still roaming loose.

Satan never reveals the results of sin. MLM looks quite alluring on the surface. You never see the destruction that it has caused, the pain inflicted on the spouse, the disappointed and ignored children. The enemy just lets you see the glitter. It appeals to your senses and leads you down the road to bankruptcy, destroyed friendships, and defeat. Florence Bulle adds:

> Being a Spirit-filled Christian does not make one immune to the [d]evil's trickery. So it's crucial to shape up, spy out the [e]nemy's strategy, and give attention to the battle being waged. This means confronting the popular theologies of our day and scrutinizing

them in the light of the Scriptures. When we do, we may be shocked to discover how many turn out to be not so biblical after all.[10]

We Accept False Teaching

There are models of thought that set forth a theology of the spoken word. Commonly known as *positive confession*, it could also be called *thought actualization*. This belief emphasizes the inherent power of words and thoughts. If you have lingered at the table where this false doctrine is fed week after week, you are a prime target for MLM.

Some who teach this doctrine argue that just as God, by His faith, conceived of the creation in His mind and brought it forth into existence by His spoken word (Gen. 1; Ps. 33:6; Heb. 11:3; 2 Pet. 3:5), so the Christian can conceive of things or images in his mind and actually bring them into existence by faith-activated words. It's called the *gospel of wealth*. Prosperity preacher Frederick Price states it this way:

> It's a matter of your faith. You got one dollar faith, and you ask for a ten thousand dollar item—it ain't gonna work. It won't work. Jesus said, "According to your faith," not "according to His will if He can work it into His busy schedule." He said, "According to your faith be it unto you." Now I may want a Rolls Royce and don't have but bicycle faith. Guess what I'm gonna get? A bicycle.[11]

Central to the gospel of wealth is this: The financial prosperity of every Christian is God's will. Therefore, a believer living in poverty is outside God's intended will. If you believe this, it's easy to see why you would also believe the MLM allure. After all, since we are God's children and His will for His children is wealth, we should always go first-class. We should have the biggest and the best. Only this brings glory to God!

If our theology treats God as if He were simply involved in our lives to fulfill our every wish, to cater to our every whim, we now have a God who is there to do *our* will, not us to do *His*. So which is it? Does He serve us, or are we to serve Him?

Many of us have heard TV evangelists make statements like: "God is love, and His will is for you to enjoy wealth and prosperity. He wants you rich. He owns the cattle on a thousand hills. Would an earthly millionaire make his own children eat poor food, wear shabby clothes, and ride in a broken-down family car? Of course not! Neither will your heavenly Father give you anything but the very best! What is the desire of your heart? Name it, claim it by faith, and it's yours!" We forget that the difficulties of this life work God's design and character in us. It's far too difficult to be quiet, rest, and wait for God to work in our lives. It seems much easier for us to act, even if we bring ourselves more stress and trouble when doing so.

Have we accepted what could be MLM's slant on Psalm 23?

The Lord is my banker; my credit is good. He maketh me to lie down in the consciousness of omnipresent abundance; He giveth me the key to His strongbox; He restoreth my faith in His riches; He guideth me in the paths of prosperity for His name's sake. Yea, though I walk in the very shadow of debt, I shall fear no evil, for Thou art with me; Thou preparest a way for me in the presence of the collector; Thou fillest my wallet with plenty; my measure runneth over. Surely goodness and plenty will follow me all the days of my life, and I shall do business in the name of the Lord forever.[12]

We Take Things into Our Own Hands

We think we could make it if we just had the right opportunity. If we could just get the right attitude or work harder. Perhaps MLM is the missing piece. And if it doesn't quite fit? Well, with just a little effort on your part, your upline will help you make it fit.

We Fail to See God in Our Negative Circumstances

It's easy to believe every negative circumstance in our life is the devil's fault. Then we think we need to counter every setback, pull ourselves up by our bootstraps, and come against any resistance or negative situation. We then easily cross the line and think that our boss is a jerk, that we're not being appreciated, that we are in a work situation that does not allow us to be who we are in God. We blame the devil when God is refining us, putting us in situations that bring all the dross in our heart to the surface. If we would only submit to Him and say, "Yes, Lord! What are You trying to teach me in these trying circumstances?" how much farther along we would be.

We Don't Take Our Needs to the Cross

In *Consumed by Success* I wrote about my need for approval. Nothing mattered to me quite as much as gaining attention and a compliment from my father. Even as an adult—yes, even as a Christian—I longed for approval. I craved attention, and MLM gave me both. I had not taken those inner needs to the cross. Did I know Jesus? Most certainly. But I still had the inner drive to fulfill those hidden needs. Only when I took them to the cross while I was breaking free of the sweet deceit of MLM did I recognize both the need and the answer to those needs.

We Neglect God's Word

One cannot help but see how important it is to base our attitudes on the truth of God's Word, "For the love of money is the root of all evil: which while some coveted after, they have erred from the faith, and pierced themselves through with many sorrows" (1 Tim. 6:10 KJV). How much of a scholar does a person need to be to understand that passage?

Peter warns us about false teachers who will draw many away with devious methodology, greed, exploitation, and sensuality (2 Pet. 2:1–3).

The warnings are clear and very understandable. But when we neglect God's Word—when we look for answers to life's struggles and problems elsewhere first—we are vulnerable.

We Don't Use Good Sense or Ask for Discernment

Didn't you notice that new MLM recruits are encouraged to deny any thought that is different than those of the presenters?

How many times have you assumed the blame because you were hesitant or had second thoughts? Did you ask questions? Why not? Afraid you might be perceived as being too critical? Did you assume that no one would understand your point of view or be threatened by different opinions than those presented? Did you shame yourself into thinking you were just being too suspicious or afraid of taking a risk?

We may not want to believe it, but it's true: A person can lose a correct perception of reality because the only reality allowed at the recruitment and motivational meetings is that of the presenter's. All other perceptions are disqualified and discouraged.

When we fail to check into our discernment, we are more susceptible to the hype and deception MLM presents to new recruits.

We Fail to Think

Think about it. At some point, didn't you suspect down deep inside that there really could be deception going on? Didn't you notice how the group pressure pulled you along through the indoctrination process until you finally accepted the belief system that promised you unlimited opportunity to become wealthy? What happened to your independent, critical thinking ability?

Put both your thinking and discernment into gear. Wake up and realize that the same tactics used to indoctrinate people into cults are practiced in many MLM recruitment and motivational meetings.

We Doubt That a Christian Might Lead Us Astray

"I have a word from the Lord for you. . . ." Be careful, it may be the deceiver speaking! We've already recognized that we may have been neglecting God's Word. Let's not make that mistake again. Christians can lead other Christians astray. It happens all the time. And, what's more, we were warned. "I send you out as sheep in the midst of wolves" (Matt. 10:16).

"Take note," say ministers and authors David Johnson and Jeff VanVonderan. "Where are the wolves? They're in the house! A concerned apostle Paul, in preparing to leave Ephesus, says in Acts

20, 'I know that after my departure savage wolves will come in among you, not sparing the flock; and from among your own selves men will arise' (v. 20)."[13]

While you probably don't feel unspiritual for locking the door to your house, you would probably feel very unspiritual for saying, "No, thank you" to a fellow Christian who asked if they could give you a word from the Lord.[14]

If a fellow Christian comes to you with a "word from the Lord," and that word includes an incredibly wonderful opportunity to make more money than you ever dreamed before—and if that deal includes making the messenger wealthy as well—do more than just say no thank you: *Run!*

We Refuse to Believe Shepherds Would Exploit Their Sheep

Most of the destruction done to the flock is done by shepherds, not just other sheep. It can be hard to believe, but there are wolves disguised not only as sheep, but shepherds who can and do devour the flock in hopes of making a fast buck. Some of these "shepherds" have led entire flocks of sheep down the path of destruction. In *The Subtle Power of Spiritual Abuse,* Johnson and Van-Vonderan say it this way: "Beware of these false prophets, Jesus warned in Matthew 7:15. The wolves are in the house and some of them are in charge."[15]

One entire Northern California congregation was destroyed because the pastor was pushing his favorite long-distance telephone service. When his congregational leaders balked at the use of his influence to sign up people under him, he simply resigned the church and took his congregational downline with him and started another church nearby. His Sunday night services routinely became praise, worship, and recruitment meetings. Eventually the sheep got tired of being used for the shepherd's profit. Some of them drifted back to the former church; some just drifted away from the church altogether.

Just like a religious cult, MLM can make its clergy loads of money. Unfortunately, it's a very different story for the followers.

We Give in to Pressure

Everybody knows what it's like to buy a candy bar from a child raising money for soccer uniforms. Who hasn't bought cookies to help out the Girl Scouts? Many people found themselves in an MLM program much the same way. Somebody you love, respect, or admire has signed up and wants you to sign up under him. Perhaps it's your doctor or chiropractor. Possibly it's your counselor or even a spiritual mentor. Maybe it's somebody who has the ability to make or break your ministry in the church. It could even be a parent. To refuse their MLM advances means you have to say no to someone you are used to agreeing with or submitting to. MLM presentations in that context are not just pressure but plain and simple harassment. Much like sexual harassment, it can be subtle or blatant. It is economic and emotional harassment either way. If someone who serves in your church or is a superior uses his or her position of power to encourage you to sign up in MLM, it is harassment in all its ugliness. It's the power of persuasion turbocharged with the potential for emotional abuse.

Many corporations, as well as churches, have specifically written sections in their policy and employee manuals on protection against sexual harassment. But how many churches and companies have protected themselves from other forms of harassment, including MLM?

We Allow Carnality to Tempt Us Away from God's Purpose

The Bible says: "Do not love the world or the things in the world. If anyone loves the world, the love of the Father is not in him. For all that is in the world—the lust of the flesh, the lust of the eyes, and the pride of life—is not of the Father but is of the world" (1 John 2:15–16 NKJV).

The lust of the flesh—the intoxicating power of money, the proposition of proposed independence—is very alluring, to say the least. The lust of the eyes—the dream vacations, big houses, and luxury cars—crackles with magnetism and pulls us toward the comfort of luxury and wealth. The pride of life—see how many people in my downline look to me for their motivation and a purpose for being—it's all too sweet.

Many don't even recognize the idolatry of it all. "Anything you serve besides God," says Johnson and VanVonderan, "or anything from which you derive your sense of life, value, and acceptance, is an idol."[16]

It comes down to this: We like to think it can't happen to us, but the more riches pile up, the more they tend to dim one's view of the Lord of lords. To varying degrees, the rich often become little lords, using the power and prestige associated with wealth to build and control their little kingdoms.[17]

We Refuse to Listen to Warning Signals

It's hard to realize that the very fix we're in may be the way God intends to get our attention in the first place. So thinking all that glitters must be God, we ignore the warning signals that would normally grab our attention. We convince ourselves God can't be pleased with our financial struggle or failure. "Maybe," we say to ourselves, "this MLM plan is an answer to my prayers." What prayers?

Paul Bilheimer in *Don't Waste Your Sorrows* says:

> Sometimes, to suffer failure is the only way one can be decentralized. Sometimes it is the suffering of adversity, catastrophic disaster, and utter loss that is necessary to produce the meekness, compassion, and selflessness without which one may remain unqualified for lofty eternal rank. . . . If failure works better than success to prepare a man for rulership, you can be sure that God loves him too well to shield him at the expense of his "eternal weight of glory."[18]

Don't forget, MLM promoters are masters at group psychology. At recruitment meetings, they create a frenzied, enthusiastic atmosphere where group pressure and promises of easy money play upon people's greed and fear of missing out on a good deal. It is difficult to resist this kind of appeal unless you recognize that the whole plan is rigged against you.

We Forgot That Life Is More Than Amassing Wealth

In his classic book *In the Footprints of the Lamb,* writer Gary Steinberger says:

> That which makes the men of God so great and impressive is not, first and foremost, what they have accomplished. It is rather how they are able, by God's help, to pass through the greatest difficulties and the darkest hours; when, like Abraham, they give God the dearest they have; when, like Daniel, they brave the greatest dangers; and when, like Moses, they endure that which is well nigh impossible. Thus they glorify God.[19]

Have we also forgotten the principle of self-denial? Florence Bulle asks a question we would be wise to consider.

> What if success means men and women get so caught up in their business and careers that God is pushed to the fringes? Failure—if it happens—may well be a blessing.
>
> Sometimes it takes failure to drive us to a deeper commitment than we would otherwise make. And sometimes failure serves as the motivation for us to get our priorities in line with God's. Failure is often God's discipline to keep us from going astray.[20]

Furthermore, we might forget how to be content. And it happens because we forgot greed is a sin. The Bible says, "Godliness with contentment is great gain" (1 Tim. 6:6). What would you do with all that extra cash anyway? If you believe that you would pour it all into God's work, you have forgotten that God doesn't call you into MLM; it's the fleshly enticements. Flesh rarely contributes to the work of God's kingdom. It has its own kingdom to feed and support.

> It is one thing to be blessed with wealth, to recognize that all one has is from God, and to be a righteous steward of those blessings. It is quite another to hold the attitude, "I have the right to be rich!" Moreover, when someone defends an indulgent lifestyle, a

look behind the scenes may reveal that accumulated wealth is often at the expense of the less fortunate.[21]

We Want It to Happen

We want it to work, we want it to be right, and we want to believe that everything that glitters so gloriously must be God. And yet, James didn't identify with the affluent, but he did have a word for them: "Now listen, you rich people. Your wealth has rotted. Your gold and silver are corroded. Their corrosion will testify against you. . . . You have hoarded wealth in the last days. You have lived on earth in luxury and self-indulgence" (James 5:1–5).

We have to ask why the God-wants-you-rich prophets don't take their message where it is needed most. Compared to millions around the world, the persons whom they address are already wealthy. But they shrug and say, "Wealth is relative, of course, a matter of degree. And we have needs in our culture that others don't have."

> But you and I need to remember that not all the King's kids are dressed in suits and ties, fancy dresses, or designer jeans. This very hour, brothers and sisters in Christ are suffering in deprivation, torture, and even martyrdom. Considering this, I cringe whenever a church leader who lives in unrestrained luxury says that prosperity is God's stamp of approval on his life and work![22]

The enemy still roams throughout the whole earth, seeking whom he may devour. You and I can no longer consider ourselves lucky, fortunate, or blessed when we stumble into what looks like something glittery and glorious and might be "from the Lord." These are the very days the Bible warns us about when it says, "For the time will come when men will not put up with sound doctrine. Instead, to suit their own desires, they will gather around them a great number of teachers to say what their itching ears want to hear. They will turn their ears away from the truth and turn aside to myths" (2 Tim. 4:3–4).

The dreams and allure of MLM are a myth. It has no substance to it. Many of its victims are still wondering what happened and blaming themselves.

"But you," the Bible says, "*You* keep your head in all situations, endure hardship, do the work of an evangelist, discharge all the duties of your ministry" (2 Tim. 4:5).

For many MLMers the truth is hard to face. The reality of the truth is as harsh as a bright light switched on in your face in the dark of night. Our first inclination is to turn away, to shut our eyes against the brightness of truth. But it won't work. God doesn't give up on us that easily. He didn't give up on me, and He won't give up on you.

The Moment of Truth

What does it take for some people to realize that MLM is a tragic mistake? As many as 99 percent of MLM recruits fail in their start-up attempt. One man posted on the Internet that ten out of the top twenty opportunities picked by *Success* magazine in March 1992 were no longer in business. If one out of every two opportunities turned sour, and if ninety-nine out of one hundred recruits quit within their first year, why aren't more people bailing out of MLM? Why are so many still willing to give it a try? It's the addictive quality of the illusion of making it big despite the failures and warnings. People just don't want to see the real picture.

No matter how we try to expose and uncover the truth, many will keep on being deceived. Their moment of truth has not yet arrived. But for you the deceit of

MLM has been unmasked. Your moment of truth has arrived.

MLM promises unbelievable opportunities. You believed them, but no longer. Now you understand that the whole dream-based reality only leads to destruction and devastation of your energy and family. Even your church could be in danger. But there is hope. You have faced the truth and are on your way to freedom. You have the hope of getting your life back. And, what's more, you're not alone!

More and more dedicated Christians are seeing the light. One by one they are facing the fact that MLM does more harm than good.

That's what happened to Beryl.

> I read Athena's article. . . . Afterward, I was convinced: Any true seeker after God would not touch multi-level marketing with a ten-foot pole! Yet I realize that many true seekers after God, including myself, are involved with MLM. We have been so deceived!

And also to Janine.

> I've just finished reading your book, *Consumed by Success,* and wanted you to know how the Lord used it in my life. Although I've never been really motivated to make it to the top, I have made several attempts at MLM in my desire to work from home in my own business. After the last big flop in 1991, I swore off trying to make it in MLM. Then, a few months ago, I became interested in still another MLM. This one sounded different. The company didn't really push people to recruit and build an organization. However, in spite of a check in my spirit, I went ahead. Once again I fell into old habits. Instead of letting my business build slowly, enthusiasm led me to overstock my inventory. When classes were canceled or postponed, I found myself up against all kinds of roadblocks and frustrations. I can't tell you of the depression and guilt that followed. I have finally learned that even those of us who aren't top leaders in MLM can sin by trying to provide by our own means instead of trusting God. Through prayer, Scripture, sermons and lessons at church, and your book,

God has shown me that I've been trying to manage my own life instead of trusting Him day by day.

Cathi's story isn't that much different.

I felt like an idiot! When I finally opened my eyes, I saw a bunch of burnt-out, grumpy egomaniacs, fighting amongst themselves and looking not at all like I saw them at the conventions and motivational meetings. They sure didn't sound like I'd heard them on their tapes! I asked myself if this was where I was going and if these were the people I wanted to go with. The answer was no! I decided to quit. My upline, like so many before him, had run out of money and dropped out. His upline made me all kinds of promises, so I had stayed. His success, after all, depended on the efforts of workaholics like me lower down the line. The dream had turned into a nightmare.

THE MOMENT OF TRUTH—A NEW OPPORTUNITY

Given the right set of circumstances, the golden opportunity to hear God speak clearly and decisively will come. All it takes is a turn of events, an unguarded moment when the Holy Spirit seizes an opening into a receptive heart.

My moment of truth came unexpectedly. Like I wrote in *Consumed by Success:*

For the first time in years I felt an overwhelming urge to pray. Prayer was my last resort these days. But that weekend, as I quietly spent time in prayer, the Lord took me back to July of 1991. I felt compelled to dig out that journal entry. I had gone off in another direction, just because it sounded good! I had assumed that, because I saw an open door, I should go through it. The Lord was making it undeniably clear that just because that door was open did not mean He wanted me to walk through it![23]

Right there in my journal were the words in my own familiar handwriting. On that particular summer day, I had been impressed that this was to be a season of rest and quietness—to learn to make my husband and children my priority and ministry. "Unhurried and unharried," I had written. "To be at peace and at one with the Lord."

As I reread what the Lord had given me, I felt a wave of conviction wash over me. For the first time in three years, I was confronted with the strong feeling that I had been in complete disobedience by getting back into MLM. It was as clear as the ink in my journal. God had told me what to do, and I had not obeyed.

There in my journal I had documented the fact that I was sensing a renewed call to ministry but only after a season of peace and rest. Nothing could be more opposite to that direction than involvement in MLM. I had recorded my inner thoughts mingled with deep spiritual insight. God had spoken to me clearly, understandably. I had not listened. He wanted me so quiet and rested in Him that He would be able to speak to me even in a whisper. Yet, ignoring His call, I rebuffed His invitation. I desired to do my own thing, without even realizing it. At that very same time Chuck and I had made a renewed commitment to live by faith—to trust God at a level beyond our ability, depending on Him entirely. How interesting that even though I had made that commitment in my mind I could still justify getting involved in MLM again!

Interestingly enough, that was not the last entry in my journal. But after that, my entries changed. Looking back and going through those pages, I saw that my prayers changed from speaking to God and listening in prayerful quietness to writing down my prayers without waiting or listening for His voice. No wonder I fell for the allure again.

That day in June 1994, I faced my moment of truth—that particular point in time when I saw my error and independence. Such realization came with the painful awareness of having failed God. Then I became conscious of how I had failed Chuck and the commitment to faith we had made together. That moment of comprehension brought me to my knees. I understood exactly what I had to do next: I had to repent.

Many things led up to my Damascus Road experience. The first and most devastating was when the company I had pledged my loyalty to had proven that it lacked integrity by changing the compensation plan. On the heels of that devastating blow, problems cropped up with the product. People got sick all across the country from inferior ingredients that were used to cut costs. Again the company had proven itself to be lacking ethics. During my first few years with the company, the Lord had tried in many small ways to get my attention—months where no one got paid, constant home-office management turnover, problems with governmental agencies, and the like. But I was sold. All those problems just had to be the devil trying to steal my dream. Finally, I realized that maybe it wasn't the devil after all. God was trying to get my attention . . . and now He finally had it!

The following days and weeks were terrible. I decided to face my upline, inform my downline, and walk away from my business rather than continue to keep propping it up. I went cold turkey, no looking back. Exposed to the holiness of God and His patient dealing with me as His child, I stopped doing MLM. Just like that. I had to let it all come crashing down. I determined that no matter what our financial condition, I never again wanted anything in my life that was not God's perfect will. I had new understanding of the words, "There is a way that seems right to a man, but its end is the way of death" (Prov. 14:12). I never, ever want to taste that much self-inflicted pain again.

Don't Miss Your Moment of Truth

How can you recognize the moment of truth? Ask yourself some really tough questions. Start with these:

- Have I abandoned being around people who are hungry for God?
- Have I given up church services in my own church, easing my conscience with MLM-sponsored church services?
- Have I violated Proverbs 12:26, which says, "A righteous man is cautious in friendship, but the way of the wicked leads them astray"?

- Have I been careless with relationships, choosing friends just for business benefit?
- Have I damaged relationships in building my MLM business? With whom?
- Have I ever dropped anyone, severed a relationship, or moved on because someone wasn't interested in being part of my organization?
- Have I ever avoided others because they were critical or nonsupportive of my MLM activity?
- Do I find myself looking forward to the next motivational tape, conference, or meeting with my upline more than I enjoy actually selling my product?
- Do I need the dream to keep me enthused and motivated on a daily basis?
- Have I fallen into a devotional pattern that concentrates only on scriptures promising blessings, abundance, and prosperity?
- Have I adopted a success mentality that justifies the means by the end?
- Have I developed the habit of praying only for what *I* want—*my* goals, *my* dreams, *my* agendas and ambitions—rather than simply praying, "*Your* will be done"?
- Have I come to believe that MLM is my only answer for financial success and happiness?
- Have I decided that God is going to use my talents and God-given gifts in MLM based on the fact that they seem a perfect fit?
- Have I begun to live my life with the attitude that it's easier to ask forgiveness than it is to ask permission?

If this book has brought you to your moment of truth, don't shut it out. You could waste this moment, and God would have to find still another way to bring you this truth. The only way to break the power of MLM's stronghold is repentance. Open the eyes of your heart to see the truth. ". . . do you show contempt for the riches of his kindness, tolerance, and patience, not realizing that

God's kindness leads you toward repentance?" (Rom. 2:4). Experience for yourself the kindness of God as you come to Him in repentance. Keep also in mind the consequence of turning once again to your own way. "But because of your stubbornness and your unrepentant heart, you are storing up wrath against yourself for the day of God's wrath, when his righteous judgment will be revealed" (Rom. 2:5).

Repent from the ungodly and destructive way of thinking that led you into MLM in the first place. God is gracious, tender toward you, and full of mercy. He waits to hear your prayer. Then rejoice like the Psalmist when he said, "Praise be to the LORD, for he has heard my cry for mercy. The LORD is my strength and my shield; my heart trusts in him, and I am helped" (Ps. 28:6–7).

Strength for the Days Ahead

There are going to be difficult days ahead. I wish I could tell you that once you repent of your involvement with MLM everything will suddenly smooth out and your difficulties will part before you like the Red Sea. It isn't going to happen. There's still a lot of work to be done. God will do His part; you will do your part. Together you will accomplish miraculous things.

Just remember God's Word:

> To you, O LORD, I called; to the LORD I cried for mercy: "What gain is there in my destruction, in my going down into the pit? Will the dust praise you? Will it proclaim your faithfulness? Hear, O LORD, and be merciful to me; O LORD, be my help." (Ps. 30:8–10)

> Do not withhold your mercy from me, O LORD; may your love and your truth always protect me. For troubles without number surround me; my sins have overtaken me, and I cannot see. They are more than the hairs of my head, and my heart fails within me. Be pleased, O LORD, to save me; O LORD, come quickly to help me. (Ps. 40:11–13)

Remember this: I can do *everything* through him who gives me strength (Phil. 4:13).

My Second Moment of Truth

Once I had realized that God did not want me in any way involved in MLM, I extricated myself and went on to a career in publishing with my husband. But God was not through with me. In 1995, He made it clear that I was to write my story in what became *Consumed by Success*. His mandate was clear: Warn the Body of Christ. My first edition was a ninty-six-page account of my experience in MLM, how God showed me that I was wrong, and how I allowed the breaking that the Lord needed to do in my heart.

Shortly after the book came out, I met a crown ambassador (the highest level upline in one of the largest MLM organizations in the world) for lunch. She had just been through a divorce and was reeling. She had read my book and admitted that everything I had said was true, even in her organization, one that held itself up as a Christian organization. At one point, it became obvious that, even though she could see the problems with MLM, she wanted to believe that she could change it from within. She didn't want to walk away from her security blanket, regardless of the compromise involved. She knew I was going to be revising and expanding the first edition and asked if there was some way I could admit that MLM is OK for some people as long as they pray about it and stay balanced and don't get consumed. I prayed, and what the Lord began to reveal to me was not what she had been hoping for.

I Am My Brother's Keeper

My second moment of truth just could not be ignored. I came to the undeniable truth: The MLM system itself is faulty. There is no way I could encourage any Christian to be involved in any facet of this industry. The fact that the system is full of compromise and flesh, no matter how much good comes of it, cannot be ignored. No matter how wonderful the product or service may be, the bottom line is you must recruit and build a downline in order to make money. Therefore, you must begin to view people as those who fall into one of two categories: those who will or will not help you in that task. People then become the means to an end, rather than the end.

Even if we can keep our MLM business in balance and work it only fifteen hours a week, the minute we sign up someone into our downline they go into the company's database. Now they're on the mailing list. All the company propaganda highlighting rags to riches stories will now be sent directly to them. Every new contest to bolster sales will arrive at their home. Every new video or audio presentation will be sent directly to them. The company's presentations exposing the frustration of corporate America and giving the solution of MLM will now land on that person's doorstep. Even if you do not use those manipulative tactics, the companies do, and they'll do it for you. You will influence others to be enmeshed in a system that you cannot support. Consider Matthew 18:6:

> But whoever causes one of these little ones who believe in me to stumble, it would be better for him to have a heavy millstone hung around his neck, and to be drowned in the depth of the sea.

The prosperity doctrine and MLM philosophy of building your future with the free-enterprise system will permeate your entire organization whether you want it to or not. Your downline never really belongs to you; it belongs to the company. The fact that the compensation plan provides the most money when building a downline will tell you that that is where the focus will be from the top down. People are no longer souls; they are prospects. Again, no matter how wonderful the product is, you can't get away from the fact that the opportunity for financial success by building a company within a company is the focus. Big money is always flaunted to motivate distributors. This causes brothers and sisters in Christ to lust after the things of this world, justifying it with a plan to give to ministries. MLM becomes a counterfeit for true evangelism. If we spent the same amount of time evangelizing our neighborhoods that we spend going to MLM meetings and building our prospect list, our churches would be booming and the kingdom of darkness would be decreasing rather than increasing!

My second moment of truth had arrived, and I could no longer deny it. The conclusion was clear as a bell: Multi-level marketing is something that *every* Christian should avoid like the plague. Every time I found something about MLM that had some redeeming value, the Lord showed me another area that caused people to compromise and stumble. Then He reminded me of my motives.

This message has cost me. I made a commitment never to take any royalties from *Consumed by Success* or this book. I never wanted there to be any personal gain involved. I didn't want to do a radio interview in the evening and then go to church the next morning hoping someone heard me and wanted to buy a copy of my book. So I chose to give what profit would have normally been mine to a few different ministries. At this point, I've probably given away as many books as our publishing company has sold. The time I spend doing interviews is not a moneymaking proposition. I don't get paid for that time, and I don't take royalties from the books that sell from the interviews. This is a calling on my life. God has given me a hard word for the Body of Christ. He has commissioned me to warn people. This is not a message that many people like to hear, especially those committed to the MLM way of life. But I'm not preaching this message to score points with man, but with God.

Regardless of what you believe about MLM, please allow the Lord to show you if it is wrong for you. Your decision will help you as you draw closer and closer to the One who loves you. He died for you and wants an intimate relationship with you—not for what He can give you but for who He is.

Part Two:
Breaking Free

Breaking free is not easy; it will take work, patience, and spiritual vigilance. You will have to guard your heart and protect your mind. You will have to stand against criticism and remain firm in the face of misunderstanding. After all, you didn't get where you are over-night, and you won't get through it by morning either. I know firsthand what you're facing.

Let me urge you to make some careful steps to diligently move toward freedom, wholeness, and restoration. The next few short chapters are important. Don't rush or skim through them. Each step will help you claim your freedom.

1

Slow Down before You Break Down

At one point in my life, I had never slowed down enough to let the Lord heal areas in me that were causing workaholism and dysfunction. I worked six, sometimes seven days a week. As you can imagine, this schedule took its toll. Once God had made it clear that I could no longer be involved in MLM, the motivation to make money—which had kept me going—was gone.

Suddenly, I felt useless. What was my purpose, my mission in life? Many days I didn't even dress until late in the afternoon. Guilt and remorse left me deeply depressed and lethargic. Emotionally decimated, I barely functioned. All my strength was gone. I had no interest in the business, no desire to compete or achieve or impress anyone. I couldn't even pray.

Allowing people and circumstances to overwhelm me, I experienced firsthand what Watchman Nee refers to as the wearing-down tactics of Satan. Once the burnout set in and I lost my motivation to succeed, the enemy had a heyday whispering accusations and filling my mind with fear. This seemed to go on for months as I wondered what would become of me. Finally, I discovered the quiet, whispered voice of God. And He had plenty to say!

As difficult as it was for me to admit, I finally realized that I had worked myself into a lifestyle where I felt perfectly capable of handling everything and everyone. Although I had ignored nagging doubts, I was nearly unable to face the fact that I had stopped growing in my understanding of God. Trying to serve God and yet ignore truth doesn't work. I had been living my life as if God didn't even notice my disobedience and distance from Him.

It is possible to be so caught up in the pursuit of success that we squeeze the very presence of God right out of our lives. Have you done that? Have you let the promise of success become so important to you that you have chosen accomplishment over intimacy with your heavenly Father? Only returning to quietness and rest before Him will show if it's true.

In his book, *Ordering Your Private World*, Gordon MacDonald urges us to rest. "Most of us think of resting as something we do after our work is done. But Sabbath rest is not something that happens after. It may in fact be something that is pursued before."[24] I urge you, stop. Before you attend another motivational meeting or recruit someone else into your organization or make one more sales presentation—stop! Let God speak to you about the rest He plans and intends for His children. And in that rest consider Him. Ask Him if this is really how He wants you spending your life. Is this His will for you?

Take the time to revisit your belief in Christ, to recommit yourself to His life in you. Refresh yourself in His love.

MacDonald also says, "When we rest in the biblical sense, we affirm our intentions to pursue a Christ-centered tomorrow. We ponder where we are headed in the coming week, month, or year. We define our intentions and make our dedications."[25]

Such rest is a choice. We are not driven to rest; we purpose and decide to rest. Even Jesus often sought solitude. How long has it been since you withdrew to seek God and His rest? When did you last contemplate where your life is and where it is going? How centered is your life on Jesus Christ as opposed to goals, quotas, and levels in MLM? Who is on the throne of your life? You, your business, or God? Materialism or the Master? Success or the Savior?

Listen to the Word of God:

> This is what the Sovereign LORD, the Holy One of Israel, says: "In repentance and rest is your salvation, in quietness and trust is your strength, but you would have none of it. You said, 'No, we will flee on horses.' Therefore you will flee! You said, 'We will ride off on swift horses.' Therefore your pursuers will be swift! A thousand will flee at the threat of one; at the threat of five you will all flee away, till you are left like a flagstaff on a mountaintop, like a banner on a hill." Yet the LORD longs to be gracious to you; he rises to show you compassion. For the LORD is a God of justice. Blessed are all who wait for him! (Isa. 30:15–18)

Will you slow down and in quietness trust God to show you the truth? Take some time right now to at least consider a quiet getaway.

- If I were to take some time and drive a short distance from my home to pray and think, where would I go?

    1. _____
    2. _____
    3. _____
    4. _____
    5. _____

- If I canceled everything on my calendar for tomorrow, what would actually happen to my life as a whole?

    1. _____
    2. _____
    3. _____
    4. _____
    5. _____

- What are my reasons for delaying such a getaway?

  1. _____
  2. _____
  3. _____
  4. _____
  5. _____

- How many of those reasons are really excuses?

  _____

Make these commitments:

- I will slow down, take a break, or getaway on ___/___/___.
  (date)

- In order to do that I will have to make the following arrangements:

  1. _____
  2. _____
  3. _____
  4. _____
  5. _____

Once you have chosen to take the time and have determined the place, take this book with you and work through the following steps quietly, prayerfully. Ask God to give you the courage to look at the tough issues yet ahead. Be assured of His love and care toward you. Thank Him for bringing you to this place and for bringing you this book.

Let this be a time of pursued intimacy with the Father. Can you imagine how your life would change if you spent as much time with Him as you have your upline/downline folk? What wonderful, creative ideas could you come up with if you opened your calendar to the Lord and said to Him, "It's Yours, Father. Show me what to do for You"?

Assess Your
Contentment Quotient

Are you a prime target for greed and ambition? Are you consumed with amassing worldly possessions? Or can you thank God for whatever you have, whether it's a little or a lot? Use the following questions to guide your thinking. Try to assess your present contentment quotient.

- How satisfied are you at this moment?
- Does taking time away from your business make you feel uncomfortable?
- If you actually laid aside the pursuit of wealth and abandoned the dreams of building your downline, would you feel as if you've failed?
- How disappointed would you be if your upline suddenly quit and

said they had experienced a change of heart toward MLM and were getting out?
- What makes you feel worthwhile and productive?
- What does it take for you to be happy?

How does Philippians 4:12 compare to your life?

I have learned the secret of being content in any and every situation, whether well fed or hungry, whether living in plenty or in want.

What about 1 Timothy 6:6–11?

. . . godliness with contentment is great gain. For we brought nothing into the world, and we can take nothing out of it. But if we have food and clothing, we will be content with that. People who want to get rich fall into temptation and a trap and into many foolish and harmful desires that plunge men into ruin and destruction. For the love of money is a root of all kinds of evil. Some people, eager for money, have wandered from the faith and pierced themselves with many griefs. But you, man of God, flee from all this, and pursue righteousness, godliness, faith, love, endurance, and gentleness.

Based on your answers to the questions in this step, how contented are you? Be honest and write out your answer in a prayer to God.

Face the Truth

Ask yourself what MLM has done to your personal integrity and relationships.

Now that you have refreshed yourself in the love of God, let the truth of His life within you overpower you. Let His tenderness toward you overwhelm your fears and calm all the anxiety you have about your life, your business, and your future. Know His closeness once again. Then, enveloped in His love and mercy, ask Him to reveal the truth to you. Don't settle for anything less than the total truth about your life. Where have you strayed off His course and abandoned His pathway?

In one of the most exciting studies of our time, Henry T. Blackaby, in the *Experiencing God* devotional, urges us with these words:

> Your life is the sum responses you have made toward God. Once God

makes Himself known to you, what you do next is your decision. Your reaction reflects what you believe about Him.

The rich young ruler could not bring himself to obey, and Scripture tells us that he "went away sorrowful." You are faced with the same question as the rich young ruler. What adjustments are you willing to make in order to respond positively to Christ?[26]

Are you willing to make adjustments in your beliefs about MLM if the Holy Spirit asks you to? How about getting a different job? Could you walk away if that's what the Lord revealed was His will for you?

I am not a stranger to the emotions you are facing. I remember the knot in my stomach and the sweaty palms I had when I faced the truth. Letting go of control was terrifying! Letting God assume control of my entire life was both exciting and frightening all at the same time. But I had to face the truth. There was no way I was going to repeat the mistake of the rich young ruler in Matthew 19:16–26.

As excruciating as it was to let go, I determined to obey what God was showing me. More than anything else, I wanted His plan and purpose for my life. Chuck was overwhelming in his support.

Secure in the love of my husband and the Lord, I stopped. I no longer wrote the monthly newsletter, held opportunity meetings, or supervised training meetings. I didn't organize any more cooperative advertising programs—in short, I quit making things happen. It's not easy giving up being responsible for everyone else, but I decided to be obedient to what I felt God was showing me. I had to trust God at a level unknown before.

I am ecstatic to report to you that God hasn't let me down! Somehow His love supported me through those first difficult days and weeks. And He'll be there for you, too. Once you give your life to Him, whether for the first time or again, He will come to your side and provide all you need.

Your personal integrity will be reinstated. Damaged relationships will be restored in time. All you have to do is face the truth.

No more pipe dreams for me. How about you? Like the rich young ruler, experiencing God can be challenging.

- What challenging things is God saying to you right now?

  1. _____
  2. _____
  3. _____
  4. _____
  5. _____

- How are you choosing to respond to God?

  1. _____
  2. _____
  3. _____
  4. _____
  5. _____

- What things in your life need changing?

  1. _____
  2. _____
  3. _____
  4. _____
  5. _____

- What adjustments are you going to have to make?

  1. _____
  2. _____
  3. _____
  4. _____
  5. _____

- Whom can you turn to for support?

	NAME	PHONE
1.	_____	_____
2.	_____	_____
3.	_____	_____
4.	_____	_____
5.	_____	_____

- Who will challenge your desire to change?

	NAME
1.	_____
2.	_____
3.	_____
4.	_____
5.	_____

- Who will understand?

	NAME	PHONE
1.	_____	_____
2.	_____	_____
3.	_____	_____
4.	_____	_____
5.	_____	_____

- Who will *not* understand?

	NAME
1.	_____
2.	_____
3.	_____
4.	_____
5.	_____

- What do you need from God right now?

  1. _____
  2. _____
  3. _____
  4. _____
  5. _____

Consider How You Really Want to Live Your Life

When was the last time you actually knew your mission in God's kingdom? Once my successful ways of doing business—the way of life that had made us thousands upon thousands of dollars—were exposed to the holiness and mercy of God, I knew there was no going back. Even with an uncertain financial future, I determined never again to allow anything in my life that was not well within God's perfect will.

Yes, as hard as it may be to believe, with my life lying around me in shambles, I actually had the freedom to consider what God wanted for my life. I never again would settle for a mere good idea. After all, I had lived my life from one good idea to the next. Creativity wasn't ever in short supply. Many of my good ideas paid off and made money. But were they God's ideas? Certainly not. I probably sound like a broken record because I keep coming back to this scripture, but it is so appropriate. Proverbs 14:12 says it like this; "There is a way that seems right to a man, but its end is the way of death."

It wasn't easy. With the motivation to make money ripped out of me, I felt useless. I didn't know how to walk in the freedom of discovering God's will. It took time—several months, in fact. There were days when I felt like a failure. Although I knew what I wasn't going to do, I didn't yet know my mission in life. I didn't know where I fit into God's plan. Depression and confusion severely tested my decision to follow God's will. Feeling like a loser and a fraud challenged my worth and left me wondering if God had any purpose for me at all. For three months I felt hollow and phony, convinced I had absolutely nothing to offer at all.

"But," the Bible says,

> Because of his great love for us, God, who is rich in mercy, made us alive with Christ even when we were dead in transgressions—it is by grace you have been saved. And God raised us up with Christ and seated us with him in the heavenly realms in Christ Jesus, in order that in the coming ages he might show the incomparable riches of his grace, expressed in his kindness to us in Christ Jesus. (Eph. 2:4–7)

All the time I was in MLM, seeking earthly riches, God desired to give me the incomparable riches of His grace, to express His kindness to me in Christ Jesus. That's how I really want to live my life: as a grace-filled, saved, blood-bought woman of God; redeemed, transformed, and seated with Christ. Underneath the entrenched desires for worldly possessions, power, and wealth, was a much deeper, more precious desire to know and experience God's grace.

> For it is by grace you have been saved, through faith—and this not from yourselves, it is the gift of God—not by works, so that no one can boast. (Eph. 2:8–9)

There was nothing I could do to earn or merit this way of life. No effort, no pressure, no ambitious plans could ever get it for me. Jesus died to provide it for me. I had accepted His death as penalty for my sins. He was already my Savior; now I would accept His life. I would soon discover His plan and purpose for me.

For we are God's workmanship, created in Christ Jesus to do good works, which God prepared in advance for us to do. (Eph. 2:10)

God had a plan for me, and He has one for you. To live out His plan is our choice. I made mine. How about you? Will you accept the fact that God made you, that you are His workmanship, and that you were created to do the good works God has prepared in advance for you to do? Isn't that really how you want to live your life?

- In your deepest heart of hearts, what do you think is the good work you were created for?

  _____
  _____
  _____
  _____
  _____

- If you were fully instated in that plan, how would it be reflected in your lifestyle?

  _____
  _____
  _____
  _____
  _____

- How would your lifestyle have to change to accommodate God's plan for your life?

  1. _____
  2. _____
  3. _____
  4. _____
  5. _____

- What commitment would be required of you to make those changes?

  _____
  _____

- How do you need God's help?

  1. _____
  2. _____
  3. _____
  4. _____
  5. _____

Repent

Breaking free of the unhealthy pursuit of success at any cost isn't easy. The major overhaul that the Lord needs to do on the values we have embraced comes with a personal price. That price is our pride, and pride never dies without a terrible scene. But when we choose to be open to the Lord and admit that we don't know what's best for our lives, He is faithful to meet us and to lead us with kindness toward repentance (Rom. 2:4). Only when we are completely yielded to the Lord can He accomplish His perfect will in our hearts and lives.

To repent doesn't necessarily speak of a revivalistic religious experience. Repentance is simply the act of turning around when you realize that you've been going the wrong direction. Think of yourself as a traveler heading toward a specific destination. But when you ask directions of someone familiar with the territory, he tells you that you've taken the wrong road. Imagine someone pointing you toward the right road to get to where you want to go. You get the picture, right? Heart repentance is not something in the physical world but the spiritual. God has made it possible for you to get back on the right road, to get your life headed in the right direction.

Realize that the insight you have been given for needed change and repentance is a gift from God. The Holy Spirit is pointing you to a different road to get you to where God wants you to go. While it is often not a pleasant experience, it is a necessary one.[27]

Begin your repentance with a list. (There is space for your list at the end of this chapter.) Allow the Lord to bring conviction to your heart and show you the relationships, heart motives, and areas of idolatry that you have permitted to exist in the place that has rightfully belonged to Jesus. Write down whatever He shows you.

You may want to include covetousness. That is, after all, at the very heart of all the MLM promotional hype and group manipulation efforts. Next is discontent. The entire motivational side of MLM is aimed at causing you to be discontent—a direct violation of God's Word!

> Keep your lives free from the love of money and be content with what you have . . . (Heb. 13:5; Phil. 4:11–12)

Confess the sin of duplicity and manipulation. The Bible says, "Simply let your 'Yes' be 'Yes,' and your 'No,' 'No'; anything beyond this comes from the evil one" (Matt. 5:37). "Above all, my brothers, do not swear—not by heaven or by earth or by anything else. Let your "Yes" be yes, and your "No," no, or you will be condemned" (James 5:12). Also look at these words of Jesus: "He who speaks on his own does so to gain honor for himself, but he who works for the honor of the one who sent him is a man of truth; there is nothing false about him" (John 7:18).

Then confess those specific things as sin. Ask Him to show you the way to turn from those areas and how to embrace His will for your life. In other words, repent. Let the promise of 1 John 1:9

comfort and encourage you to complete repentance. "If we confess our sins, he is faithful and just to forgive us our sins and to cleanse us from all unrighteousness" (NKJV).

In this way, you have gone back to the starting point. You are now on the road to forgiveness and freedom. What a wonderful thing to realize that you have a new direction, that you are on the right road. You are breaking free of the sweet deceit of multi-level marketing at last.

MY REPENTANCE LIST

1. _____
2. _____
3. _____
4. _____
5. _____
6. _____
7. _____
8. _____
9. _____
10. _____

Look for Strongholds

One important factor you must not over-look in your walk into freedom is the second part of 1 John 1:9, ". . . and to cleanse us from all unrighteousness." Many times we simply think that confession leads us to forgiveness, which it does. Then, many assume that the cleansing is just the healing from the damage done by whatever sin has just been forgiven. That is true. And yet, if we don't realize there is far more to this promise, we set ourselves up for repeating damaging and destructive habits and patterns. In other words, we could be in this same place again and again. Don't stop at confession; press on to the cleansing stage.

Ask the Lord if unresolved issues in your life have driven you to find comfort in your business. He may show you some areas of wounding or abuse. If so, ask Him to heal your heart and expect Him to tenderly do so. You may want to seek counseling or a support group to help you work through the issues. Psalm 147:3 says, "He heals the brokenhearted and binds up their wounds." Let that be your promise. Rephrase it into your own personal prayer.

Then look for areas of strongholds in your own life. You may have tried your best to walk as a child of God's light. Yet, somehow failing to produce the fruit of that light, you have fallen into striving, workaholism, and materialism. Disillusioned, you try harder by working harder. Disappointed, you try to salve your misery instead of solving the problem. If so, you could be dealing with a stronghold.

Some of our strongholds are in place because of inner vows we made as children. Vows to accomplish more than a hated or disliked parent or relative, surpass our siblings in material goods, or secure our own futures rather than live out family patterns of need or lack. Without understanding what we have done, we can be driven from somewhere deep within that we don't fully remember or even recognize.

Other strongholds may be seated and in power because we have opened ourselves to them. Perhaps we have allowed ourselves to be influenced in a group rather than take a stand for what we know is right. This often happens in MLM. Even when the math doesn't add up or we have nagging thoughts about exploiting our friends and family, we keep quiet and let the alluring thoughts enter our minds and finally our hearts. Perhaps the blatant propaganda offends us at first, but we do nothing to remove ourselves from the environment where amassing wealth is being taught as normal, even desirable. Eventually it sounds reasonable and acceptable. Finally we buy in—a stronghold has made itself at home within our hearts and minds.

The function of any stronghold is to rob you of your free will. It will control your mentality and disarm you from thinking anything that will contradict it. It causes you to have tunnel vision, blocking out the Word of God. Left alone, it will destroy your conscience, taking your mind and finally your soul captive.

In *The Kingdom of the Cults,* Walter Martin states, "First and foremost, the belief system of the cults are characterized by closed-mindedness. They are not interested in a rational cognitive evaluation of the facts."[28]

In *Consumed by Success* I said:

> It's just as easy to be convinced about a business opportunity to the point of unhealthy closed-mindedness. Especially if you've built your world around your opportunity. Breaking free from the trap may seem like a scary thought, but please, be open, and see what the Lord might be trying to say to your heart.[29]

Linda is like many in MLM who are under the influence of strongholds.

> I really need some help concerning my unhealthy need for recognition and praise. I have a totally unhealthy need to achieve. I have been consumed by success in everything I have done! Top grades, top awards, top at all I've tried with miserable feelings at the slightest mistake. I've been the top producer in my unit with most sales. I've even gotten very good at using Scripture to confirm my MLM business building.

Anne wrote this:

> Thank you for writing such an emotional and wrenching book [*Consumed by Success*]. Your story could have been mine, with the exception that I never achieved any real success and ended up divorcing my husband, who just wasn't good MLM material. I can't tell you how unbelievably well I can relate to your story. I have since become friends with others who are recovering from the mind control that higher levels perpetrate on their downline people. It has been a real struggle. I used to pray at night that God would show me if this is what He wanted me to do. Once I saw the lies and illegalities exposed on the Internet, I realized why He didn't allow me to experience any success with it. He probably knew that once I did, I would never be able to leave it.

Josie wrote of her own personal struggles with strongholds:

After I'd been in the business a year, I was born again. I doubt the business had anything to do with that, but I credited the business's influence on my life and took it as proof that the business was from God.

Needless to say, much of those five years were filled with confusion. When I would allow myself to become consumed, I noticed flaunting, anti-God type thoughts, and it scared me so I'd back off. Again I thought something was wrong with me. Then I would have another go at it. By this time I thought the devil was interfering with my thought processes, interposing himself into something God so clearly wanted me to do—or so I thought.

Other times I just wanted the Lord so much I would put everything else aside and just bask in His presence. But it was so "unproductive" I didn't see how I could do both that and give the necessary attention to the business. So I put God on the back burner. I loved the business, the people, the tapes, and the functions. I loved the concepts and the principles. I didn't see how anything could be wrong with something so "good," especially something that talked about the Lord so much and steered people in that direction.

Then something changed. I would get all revved up at the rallies and weekend functions, as was intended. Later on I began to notice the manipulation involved: get people excited about principles that are right, such as God, country, self-determination. But then divert all that energy and enthusiasm to showing the plan. The buildup was toward God, but the commitment was made toward the business. Like a curve ball, [it dropped] away at the last minute.

I thank God for the strength to quit the business. It's been two years since I removed myself from such influence. I've never regretted it.

When talking with those in MLM who are bound by strongholds, I have found you can't reason with them. When they parrot learned phrases that create a smokescreen and distract you, you know you are confronting a stronghold. Those under the influence of such strongholds distort the Scripture to their own purpose. When you try to break through, you are the one treated as if you are in error. Perhaps you've been there yourself. You've repented, you're forgiven. Now you need the cleansing.

You see, the only way to break the power of the stronghold is the full work of repentance. If you or anyone you know is under the influence of hidden strongholds, only the Holy Spirit can reveal the truth. Only then can cleansing come for thinking that is ungodly and destructive.

My own personal stronghold was my deep desire for approval from men. This stemmed from hurts and wound in my young life. Because of a lack of quality time with my father, I looked to men for validation. The power of the spoken word in my life triggered a compulsive drive to do more, achieve more, be noticed more—especially by men. Even when I was happily married, I found myself striving to be noticed by men for my accomplishments. When I finally recognized my unhealthy behavior as a stronghold in my life, I asked the Lord to show me the root. I repented for the wrong motivations.

> For though we live in the world, we do not wage war as the world does. The weapons we fight with are not the weapons of the world. On the contrary, they have divine power to demolish strongholds. We demolish arguments and every pretension that sets itself up against the knowledge of God, and we take captive every thought to make it obedient to Christ. (2 Cor. 10:3–5)

If you are determined to break free of the sweet deceit of MLM, ask God to show you the strongholds. Write what God shows you:

1. _____
2. _____
3. _____
4. _____
5. _____

Surrender

Once Greg repented for wrong motives, he surrendered his life to God's purpose and now has new motives! He wrote the following:

> After signing up I carefully planned my strategy, and I was off and running. I learned exactly what to say and who to target for my new venture. I don't have to tell you what happened next. Soon I realized that the cycle never stops. My human nature wanted more, more, more. Financial freedom had become my master.
>
> After months of consideration and prayer, I finally came to the same conclusion you did. I cannot serve two masters: God and money. In accordance with Scripture, I, as a born-again Christian, will grow to love one and hate the other (Luke 16:13–15). I am ashamed to admit this, but

I have been more concerned with whether a prospect had the money to invest in my MLM business than if they had something more valuable—eternal life through Jesus Christ. I can no longer recruit friends, family, and associates to a worldly enterprise. My goal is to recruit souls for the kingdom of God! (see 1 John 2:15 and Matt. 6:19)

Greg is well on his way to being free from the sweet deceit of MLM. He has faced his moment of truth, repented, surrendered, and is now seeking God's will rather than his own. You can do the same.

You might also be saying, "I've never really surrendered my life to Christ." If that is the case, I can tell you this with confidence. God loves you and has a plan for your life. By surrendering your life to Him, He will take control of your life and fill you with a peace that passes all understanding. No one can get through life without falling short. Because of that fact, God sent His only Son, Jesus Christ, as a sacrifice. He was sent to die for us so that we might have life. It's not about religion; it's about relationship. God wants to have a personal relationship with you, and the only way for that to happen is through His Son. Jesus said, "I am the way, the truth, and the life. No one comes to the Father except through Me" (John 14:6 NKJV). If you feel a tugging to come into relationship with Him, just say this prayer:

Dear Jesus, I come to You today and acknowledge that I have fallen short. I've tried to run my life, and I haven't done a very good job. Please help me. I surrender my life completely to You. Please come into my heart and make me brand new. Forgive me for all my sins and wash me clean. I receive You now as my Savior, and I choose to make You the Lord of my life. Right now I commit my life into Your hands and pray that You will make me the person You created me to be. Thank You for saving me. In Jesus' name, amen.

Welcome to the family of God! Like a newborn baby, you have a lot of growing to do. Begin by reading God's Word, talking to

Him in prayer, and seeking the fellowship of other Christians. Find a Bible-believing church where you can worship and serve. You've taken the first step on a wonderful and adventurous journey, but don't stop there. Keep growing in your relationship to God.

8

Become Proactive in Your Spiritual Life

What moves you to prayer? Is it the call of God toward His children or circumstances? Do you cry out to God to know more of Him, to be closer to Him, or because you need help or strength? In other words, do you seek God's face or just His hand? Do you want to know Him or just benefit from His help? Ask yourself whether you seek God before a decision or after. Is it wisdom you want ahead of time or help in accomplishing *your* goals? Do you want to experience God or just His blessing?

If you seek God only for what He can do or give, rather than who He is, you are living a *reactive* lifestyle. Circumstances tend to dictate when we will seek God. When everything's going fine, we consult God less; when things are a bit tough, we press in for help and assistance.

But God seeks a deeper relationship with you than that. He wants to be part of your life, not just an answer to your problems. He loves you and wants only the best for you. He is also jealous over you. "Do not worship any other god, for the LORD, whose name is Jealous, is a jealous God" (Exod. 34:14).

Can you actually say that your relationship with Him has been one of love and intimacy? Do you serve God first and on purpose?

You have decided to at least explore the possibility, and hopefully you have made the decision to break free of the sweet deceit of MLM. You have slowed down, examined your heart, and let God look deep within your soul and your desires. You have repented. Now it is time to adjust your life.

Make some quality decisions to take time daily for worship, prayer, Bible study, and reflection. Your commitment to hungering and thirsting for more of Him (again, with the right motives) is top priority. You will have to create a time and a place where you cannot be disturbed. Sometimes I've had to drive to the beach, put on some worship music to soften my hard heart, and spend time with the Lord right there in my car. No phones, no pagers, no Daytimer. When I'm the only one at home, I sometimes take the phone off the hook.

The enemy does not want you to have quality time with Him, so he'll do whatever he can to distract you. The minute you purpose to pray and seek God's face, the phone will ring, the baby will cry, someone will knock at your door. You may suddenly remember things you forgot to do. You might dwell on something someone said. Don't let these distractions keep you from God's presence. Pray the blood of Jesus over your mind, will, and emotions. Ask the Lord to guard your heart and mind.

What does the enemy want to do?

- Keep us so stuck in the past or focused on the future that we can't experience God today
- Keep us from being hungry for more of God by filling us up with other things
- Keep us from prayer (sleep, distractions)

- Keep us from being filled with the Holy Spirit
- Keep us from the Word (confusion, distractions)
- Keep us from healthy fellowship with those who are hungry for more of Jesus
- Keep us from quiet times with Jesus
- Keep us from intimacy and hearing His voice
- Keep us from having a healthy fear of God
- Keep us from being dedicated to the cause (the Great Commission)
- Keep us from witnessing (by shame and condemnation)
- Bottom line, he wants to keep us from obedience because that's what shuts the door to Satan's control in our lives!

Here are some basic disciplines you need to practice on a daily basis.

1. *Put on your spiritual armor.* "Put on the full armor of God so that you can take your stand against the devil's schemes" (Eph. 6:11).

2. *Choose the will of God and refuse the will of Satan, just like Jesus did.* ". . . when Christ came into the world, he said: 'Sacrifice and offering you did not desire, but a body you prepared for me; with burnt offerings and sin offerings you were not pleased. Then I said, "Here I am—it is written about me in the scroll—I have come to do your will, O God"'" (Heb. 10:5–7).

3. *Give God full rule and reign.* "Our Father in heaven, hallowed be your name, your kingdom come, your will be done on earth as it is in heaven" (Matt. 6:9–10).

4. *Die to self.* "I tell you the truth, unless a kernel of wheat falls to the ground and dies, it remains only a single seed. But if it dies, it produces many seeds. The man who loves his life will lose it, while the man who hates his life in this world will keep it for eternal life. Whoever serves me must follow me; and where I am, my servant also will be. My Father will honor the one who serves me" (John 12:24–26).

5. *Ask God to open your eyes to see what wearing-out tactic Satan is using on you or those around you.* "Be self-controlled and alert. Your enemy the devil prowls around like a roaring lion looking for someone to devour" (1 Pet. 5:8).
6. *Ask God to show you your heart.* "Search me, O God, and know my heart; test me and know my anxious thoughts. See if there is any offensive way in me, and lead me in the way everlasting" (Ps. 139:23–24).
7. *Cry out to God and thirst for Him and only Him.* "Arise, cry out in the night, as the watches of the night begin; pour out your heart like water in the presence of the Lord" (Lam. 2:19).

Here's a daily prayer you may want to use:

I put on the belt of truth and the breastplate of righteousness, shod my feet in the preparation of the gospel of peace. I take up the shield of faith to ward off the fiery darts of the enemy. I put on the helmet of salvation so my mind will be transformed today to the mind of Christ. I take up the Sword of the Spirit, the Word of God, sharper than any two-edged sword, to wield against the enemy as well as to circumcise my own heart. And I pray in the Spirit today whenever I need to talk to God! Thank You, Lord, for Your armor. Thank You for protecting me!

I choose the will of God, and I refuse the will of Satan. Spirit of God, rule and reign in my life today. Rule and reign in my thoughts, my attitudes, my emotions, and my feelings. In every area, Lord God, I give You permission to rule and reign. I choose today to die to myself, my desires, my wants, my expectations, my life as I know it. Lord, I ask You to give me Yourself, Your desires, Your wants, Your expectations, Your life for me. I want Your will, not mine today, in Jesus' Name.

Give me eyes to see the tactics of the enemy in my life and the lives of those around me. Cause me, Lord, to see in the spirit realm rather than just in the natural realm. Lord, cause me to respond in the Spirit rather than in the flesh.

Lord God, today I pray that You would show me my heart as You see it. Lord, show me the good as well as the bad. Show me the areas You want to change in me. Lord, today I give You permission to show me what is truly in my heart so that You can begin to do the work You want to do in my heart. Lord, I yield to You today to have Your way.

God, today I want to be hungry and thirsty for more of You. Where I have been filled with myself and the things of the world, empty me out. Where I have hungered for other relationships, make me hungry for You. Lord, cause me to be desperate for more of You, in Jesus' Name!

Becoming proactive will definitely give you the strength you'll need for the next step.

9

Walk Away

Leaving behind the sweet deceit of multi-level marketing is a huge decision. Many well-meaning people have spent years cultivating their network of associates. When you sever your relationship to the organization, it affects everything. What will it take to walk away? The following gave me the courage to obey God and get out.

Find a Friend You Can Trust

Finding a safe person to talk to is absolutely essential. For me it meant acting on the total conviction in my heart that I have heard the voice of God and am going to obey. It meant going to someone who I knew could hear from God, someone who had complete integrity and plenty to lose by the advice she gave me. I needed someone who was more hungry to please God than please man.

Don't Hold Anything Back

As the words tumbled out, I felt great release. I had been so afraid for so long to say anything negative about the system. After all, the rule was "When you're up go down, and when you're down go up." In other words, you never told anyone in your downline of your doubts, your concerns, your negative feelings. You only tell your downline the up, positive things. The only person you talk to about negative things is your upline because they are supposedly more able to tell you the things you need to hear to get your attitude right. I was breaking the rule, unloading all my realizations on someone in my downline! But she was safe for me. She could understand what I had begun feeling and what I was processing.

Pray Immediately

After I confessed what I was feeling, we prayed for wisdom. We surrendered completely to the Lord and to His way in the situation. Coming into agreement with someone else was powerful.

Expect God to Hear and Answer

God moved swiftly in answer to those prayers. He confirmed that my decision was right and gave me someone to walk through my exit with. Having a support person made all the difference. She called me and prayed with me whenever the Holy Spirit brought me to her mind. Funny how that works! Her calls or visits always came when I really needed someone to come alongside and encourage me, when I felt like the bottom had dropped out. I needed to know that I was, in fact, doing the right thing.

Enlarge Your Circle of God-Hungry Friends

I joined a Bible study, a small group of people hungry for more of God. You'll need that to replace the MLM family you will lose.

Ask God for New Financial Strategies for Your Life

I began to believe God would be faithful to provide without my having to compromise. Now it's your turn. Just watch for His supply. "And my God shall supply all your need according to his riches in glory by Christ Jesus" (Phil. 4:19 NKJV).

Release, Rebuild, Restitution, Restoration

Now that you've decided to break free of MLM's sweet deceit, you will soon face the fact that some of your most important relationships may have been damaged. Your integrity may have been compromised; you exploited friends and family for personal profit. In addition to your own personal and spiritual restoration, those relationships will have to be restored as well. You'll need courage to walk through the rubble left behind by your out-of-control ambition and wealth addiction. But it is important that you make the effort to repair those relationships. Here are a few steps you might consider.

1. Prayerfully create a list of those you've harmed in building your business. Ask the Lord to bring to mind the names of those you've

exploited, and those you've dropped because they wouldn't support your business efforts and join your organization. Remember those who've tried to discourage you in your MLM activities. You probably rebuffed them as negative influences. This could be painful and take a long while. Be patient, but be determined. Your life is worth restoring to its fullest. People are important, and you will need all your friends and family supporting you as your rebuild your life. Write the list here:

1. _____
2. _____
3. _____
4. _____
5. _____
6. _____
7. _____
8. _____
9. _____
10. _____

2. Write out exactly how you hurt them. Did you ignore their advice? Did you avoid them? Did you exploit them and convince them to join your organization, causing them to override their own hesitation or reluctance? Did you lead them into MLM involvement through misinformation or half-truths? Did you make friends with the hidden agenda to recruit them into your MLM downline? Again, ask the Lord to help you identify the offense and how you may have wounded others. Write what He shows you here:

	Name:	I hurt them by:
1.	_____	_____
2.	_____	_____
3.	_____	_____

	NAME:	I HURT THEM BY:
4.	_____	_____
5.	_____	_____

3. Go to those you can. You may not be able to approach or meet with some of those on your list face to face. Let God work out the difficult ones. Whenever possible, go to the person you sinned against. Make the phone calls, set the appointments, and pursue your freedom through forgiveness and restoration. Be willing to admit your wrong. Confess your sin, repent, and ask forgiveness for abusing the relationship. Write the list of who you can go to here:

	NAME:	PHONE:	APPOINTMENT DATE AND TIME
1.	_____	_____	_____
2.	_____	_____	_____
3.	_____	_____	_____
4.	_____	_____	_____
5.	_____	_____	_____

4. Make a personal commitment to the Lord to keep pure heart motives in all future relationships. Ask Him to make you trustworthy again and to trust you once more. Give God the liberty to convict you when He sees you straying off track or back into old, exploitive habits and patterns. Write your prayer here:

_____

_____

_____

_____

_____

After you have walked through these important steps of rebuilding and restoring your relationships, you will want to refer to these pages again. The enemy of your soul will try to discourage you in your new commitment. He will try to make you believe that you've not really done what it will take to restore broken relationships. He will lie to you and tell you you're not making any progress at all and that you've failed once more. When that happens, review your commitment, renew your determination, and rely on the mercy and forgiveness of God.

Part Three: When Someone You Love Is Caught

Many of the responses to my first book have come from the loved ones who have been watching what MLM has done to their spouses, parents, siblings, or friends. Several have written wanting advice, asking how to approach those they love who are caught up in MLM.

So what do you do when someone you love is deeply involved in MLM?

You pray, forgive, check your own heart, ask God, fast (and pray some more), concentrate on what God wants to do in your life, be bold, extend grace, and then, wait.

1 | Pray

Pray, pray, and pray some more. Sometimes all we can do is pray for God to open eyes that are blind. A good example is the prayer of Paul for the Ephesians (Eph. 1:17–19). Personalize it with the name of your loved one and persevere in your prayers!

> I keep asking that the God of our Lord Jesus Christ, the glorious Father, may give [name]: the Spirit of wisdom and revelation, so that [he/she] may know him better. I pray also that the eyes of [name]'s heart may be enlightened in order that [he/she] may know the hope to which he has called [him/her], the riches of his glorious inheritance in the saints, and his incomparably great power for us who believe.

Keep on praying. Don't let your faith waver because of circumstance or what you see happening. God is at work to honor and answer your prayer. Remember the words of Jesus in Mark 11:22–24:

> "Have faith in God," Jesus answered. "I tell you the truth, if anyone says to this mountain, 'Go, throw yourself into the sea,' and does not doubt in his heart but believes that what he says will happen, it will be done for him. Therefore I tell you, whatever you ask for in prayer, believe that you have received it, and it will be yours."

Forgive

Next, guard yourself against anger, unforgiveness, and self-righteousness. Do not allow yourself the luxury of becoming bitter if they do not change immediately.

> And when you stand praying, if you hold anything against anyone, forgive him, so that your Father in heaven may forgive you your sins. (Mark 11:25)

Don't forget the promises of these passages:

> But I trust in you, O Lord; I say, "You are my God. My times are in your hands." (Ps. 31:14–15)

> The Lord is a refuge for the oppressed, a stronghold in times of trouble. Those who know your name

will trust in you, for you, LORD, have never forsaken those who seek you. (Ps. 9:9–10)

Don't forget that God is completely aware of the situation according to Matthew 6:8: ". . . your Father knows what you need before you ask him."

Perhaps you are a former MLMer who has read this book, ran right out, and also bought *Consumed by Success*. Hopefully you have let God work and move in your heart and are completely free and totally reformed. But you know many others need this message. You might have even considered buying these books by the case, ready to put them into the hands of all the people in MLM you know.

Hopefully you have stepped back a bit and wondered, *How do I approach them? What's the best thing for me to do?*

3

Check Your Own Heart

Then you need a heart check. Nothing is as obnoxious as a reformed *anything*.

Perhaps you have been a former fast-food junkie and now eat only healthy, wholesome food. You may be a former smoker who by the grace and power of God quit cold turkey. You know the type, free at last and determined to free everyone else they know and love—*immediately!* But it doesn't work that way.

Nothing will sabotage the work of the Holy Spirit in someone's life faster than a run-ahead, well-intentioned Christian on a misguided-guided, ill-timed mission. Your attitude is all important if God is to be able to use you to free others.

Remember, God chose the right time to bring you to the freedom He wanted for you. He knew just what circumstances had to be in place and how best to give you the information you needed to make difficult decisions. Give Him the time and space to do that in the lives of your loved ones, too. Keep on praying, but along with your prayers there is plenty you can do.

4 Ask

You must prayerfully ask the Lord to show you how to approach each person. There is no magic formula. Some will be open to you, some will not. Some are ready to hear this message, many are not. Ask God who He is dealing with. Then ask Him not only *how* but *when* to approach each of those He shows you. Ask Him, then pray some more!

5

Fast and Pray

One lady wrote to me: "I am married to a died-in-the-wool MLMer. It's ruining our home life and depleting our savings. He won't listen to me. How can I reach him?"

You already know I'm going to strongly urge you to pray. But let me also encourage spouses of those caught in MLM's sweet deceit to add fasting to their prayers.

Then, during those times of fasting and prayer, remember not to focus completely on that loved but misled spouse. Ask God what He wants to change in you.

That's right, *you.*

When your spouse walks away from MLM, there will be some very difficult days ahead. Are you ready? Can you be the marriage partner your husband will need when he repents? When she's bombarded with criticism from the organization, will you build your wife up? Will you support his decision when his upline and downline call, trying to talk him into staying? What strength will you need to love her through her misgivings and second thoughts? What are you willing to live without while he gathers his financial wits about him again? How can you become the encourager she needs during times of loss and depression?

My husband and family had to take over the complete running of the house because my post-MLM depression hit so deep. Do you have the strength to love your spouse if he or she hasn't the courage and strength to dress until late afternoon? Thank God, my husband did.

Concentrate on What God Wants to Do in Your Life

While you wait for God to move on your loved one, ask Him what He needs to do in you to get you ready for the changes that will come as a result of having your prayer answered. You'll be surprised at what God wants to do in you.

I know this isn't exactly what you wanted to hear, but there will also be changes in your life when your spouse comes to his or her senses. Seek counseling if necessary. Deal with your unforgiveness issues. Prepare yourself; if your spouse changes, your life will definitely change. Demonstrate your faith by being open to whatever work God begins to make you ready for the changes yet to come in your loved one or spouse.

One lady said, "I have to work on myself so that when the turnaround comes, I'll be ready."

And if it doesn't? "Then," she said, "I want to be healthy."

7

Be Bold

"Somebody in my church is recruiting my friends. What can I do?"

Nothing is quite as frustrating as knowing the truth of this message and seeing others approached, allured, and hooked into MLM while we stand on the sidelines. It's like watching a cult seduce those we love. Sadly, it can happen right in our churches and fellowship groups. Is there anything you can do?

Yes, of course. You know I'm going to say pray, right? But after you have prayed, perhaps you could seek the counsel of your pastor. Ask him if there aren't some ground rules that could be put in place concerning MLM recruiting in your church. When you see it happening, make an appointment with your pastor. Tell him you see this happening and have been praying (if you have been praying, that is!) and hope that he will take this seriously. Tell him you've seen how people can be abused and exploited in MLM situations, and ask him to consider setting up some boundaries within the church. It might take a while for it to fall into place, but some pastors have taken a stand and will not permit the flock to devour each other this way. Unfortunately, other pastors have been hurt by setting up such boundaries. Are you willing to stand by him if he makes a stand?

And if you can't make a difference? If your pastor decides there is nothing he can or should do, will you get hurt and withdraw, even change churches? Will that do any good or further relationships in the family of God?

Sometimes it's important to know you can't change everything, even when you see something is wrong or someone you love is headed in a direction that eventually can cause them only pain. Sometimes you simply have to let go.

8

Extend Grace

When this happens, you have an opportunity to grow in love. Learn true agape love and unconditionally continue in your relationships, all the while standing your ground. Once you have made your position clear, you may have to be the one who keeps the lines of communication open— the one who keeps on caring or even maintains the prayer burden alone. The truth can be told in love; you can be honest as you extend God's grace. Neither truth told in love nor honesty damages relationships that are open and healthy. It's when our own judgmentalism enters in, when our own self-righteousness or self-centered agendas conflict with the same in others that the damage occurs.

In time, the very person you know who will not heed this message may need you to be there for them. It will be a real test of your character. But will you pray for that growth to occur within you so that you'll be ready?

Wait

Finally, the Bible teaches that it is important to wait on the Lord.

> In the morning, O LORD, you hear my voice; in the morning I lay my requests before you and wait in expectation. (Ps. 5:3)

> Wait for the LORD; be strong and take heart and wait for the LORD. (Ps. 27:14)

> Be still before the LORD and wait patiently for him; do not fret when men succeed in their ways, when they carry out their wicked schemes. (Ps. 37:7)

Who knows how long it will take for your loved one to come to his or her senses? Waiting won't be easy, but if you can wait with thankfulness in your heart, it will be character building and life changing.

A Final Word

I've tried to describe some of the intangibles connected to MLM—the subtle, seductive attributes that suck us in and deceive our hearts. In order for believers to fight the good fight and work out our own salvation, we need to see things clearly. We need to know that there is a battle for our hearts, souls, minds, and strength. I've gently tried to remind you that only the Lord Jesus Christ deserves to own your heart, mind, soul, and body. We must diligently guard against anything that would rob Him of what is rightfully His.

My goal has been to give you some tools to work with—some ways to gauge whether you're on course with the high calling of Christ Jesus. At first glance, a word like this could be offensive to many. But I know in my heart it is necessary. One day, we will come face to face with Jesus. In Matthew 7:21–23 Jesus said:

> Not everyone who says to me, "Lord, Lord," shall enter the kingdom of heaven, but he who does the will of my Father in heaven. Many will say to me in that day, "Lord, Lord, have we not prophesied in your name, cast out demons in your name, and done many wonders in your name?" [or given to good causes, put on meetings where people got "saved," etc.] And then I will declare to them, "I never knew you; depart from me, you who practice lawlessness!"

We may say we are born again and we know Him, but the real question is this: Does He know us? Have we cultivated that intimacy with Him on a daily basis? Have we fully surrendered our hearts and lives to Him?

Today more than ever I am convinced that MLM is one of the most subtle and dangerous distractions to nurturing our personal relationship with Jesus. I believe it could be responsible for millions of believers coming to that day and hearing Jesus say, "I never knew you." That is why I've written this book: to serve as a warning. We must return to our first love before it's too late.

I've opened my heart and revealed to you my weaknesses, my sin, and my deception because I want you to know that even when we are sincere about a belief (even as sincere as I was about MLM), we can be sincerely wrong. My motives started out right but ended up wrong. No matter how much good I did, I was still wrong. I caused brothers and sisters to stumble, to covet, to be discontent, to focus on the things of the world. That is wrong, dead wrong. Yet I am not pointing fingers. I am simply exposing my own deception and how I bought into the sweet deceit woven through the very fabric of the MLM system in hopes that you might break free as well.

Now it's up to you. I can only bring the warning; expose my own wrong thinking; and reveal the subtleties of the approach, the allure, the hook, and the addiction of MLM. I've brought to light the sweet deceit of the entire system. But you must make the next move. You must get on your knees before the Lord and say, "I give up! Help me to hunger and thirst for You more than I do my business, my success, my dreams, and my goals." If you take just the first small step, He'll come running to meet you. And just like the father of the prodigal son, He'll cover you with the finest robe, have the fattest calf slaughtered for your welcome-home party, put a ring on your finger, and kiss your neck. He loves you, and He wants you to come home. Won't you come?

Endnotes

[1] Athena Dean, *Consumed by Success* (Mukilteo, WA: WinePress Publishing, 1996), p. 35.

[2] Ibid., p. 41.

[3] Drs. Hemfelt, Minirth, Meier, *We Are Driven* (Nashville, TN: Thomas Nelson Publishers, Inc., 1991), p. 6.

[4] Robert Fitzpatrick and Joyce K. Reynolds, *False Profits* (Charlotte, NC: Herald Press, 1997), p. 37.

[5] Ibid.

[6] Dale and Juanita Ryan, *Recovery from Addictions* (Downers Grove, IL: InterVarsity Press, 1990), p. 11.

[7] Hemfelt, Minirth, and Meier, p. 9.

[8] Ibid.

[9] Florence Bulle, *The Many Faces of Deception* (Minneapolis, MN: Bethany House Publishers, 1989), p. 24.

[10] Ibid., p. 17.

[11] Frederick K. C. Price, *Praise the Lord* TV broadcast on TBN, 21 September 1990.

[12] The presupposition of Charles Fillmore's (of Unity School of Christianity) thoughts on prosperity. H. Terris Newman, writing in *Pneuma: The Journal of the Society for Pentecostal Studies,* vol. 12, no. 1, Spring 1990, p. 45, records Fillmore's rendition of Psalm 23.

[13] David Johnson and Jeff VanVonderan, *The Subtle Power of Spiritual Abuse* (Minneapolis, MN: Bethany House Publishers, 1991), p. 35.

[14] Ibid., p. 47.

[15] Ibid., pp. 35–36.

[16] Ibid., p. 47.

[17] Bulle, p. 29.

[18] Paul Bilheimer, *Don't Waste Your Sorrows* (Fort Washington, PA: Christian Literature Crusade, 1977), pp. 43–44.

[19] G. Steinberger, *In the Footprints of the Lamb* (Minneapolis, MN: Bethany House Publishers, 1936), p. 28.

[20] Bulle, p. 37.

[21] Ibid., p. 30.

[22] Ibid., p. 28.

[23] Dean, p. 77–78.

[24] Gordon MacDonald, *Ordering Your Private World* (Nashville, TN: Oliver-Nelson, Thomas Nelson, Inc., 1985), p. 174.

[25] Ibid., p. 168.

[26] Henry T. Blackaby and Richard Blackaby, *Experiencing God Day-by-Day* (Nashville, TN: Broadman & Holman Publishers, 1997), p. 102.

[27] Gordon MacDonald. *Rebuilding Your Broken World* (Nashville, TN: Thomas Nelson Publishers, 1988), p. 156.

[28] Walter Martin, *The Kingdom of the Cults* (Minneapolis, MN: Bethany House Publishers, 1985), p. 26.

[29] Dean, p. 165.

Glossary

allure. The too-good-to-be-true possibilities that are presented in an opportunity meeting for an MLM.

approach. Any one of numerous methods that an established MLM individual can use to address a possible recruit.

compensation plan. This is how money is distributed in a multi-level organization. It usually depends on the volume of personal sales and the volume of organizational sales within a set time period. Everyone has a minimum quota they must maintain. Typically, compensation plans protect the company from paying out too much money. The truth is often exaggerated during the presentation of the compensation plan to a new recruit.

distributor. This status allows an individual to acquire products or services at 20 to 40 percent below suggested retail prices. The fee for becoming a distributor is typically $20 to $50 initially and then $10 to $25 per year to stay active. Some companies have no distributor fees; others waive them for a short period of time to fuel recruiting.

downline. This includes anyone who is on a lower level in the organization—all the people an individual is responsible for recruiting, whether the individual personally recruited them or someone below them did the recruiting.

dream, the. It has many faces: a future of financial independence; luxurious living; the ability to make decisions without having to ask, "How much will it cost?" The good life—a beautiful home, a nice car, a nice wardrobe, annual vacations in Maui, a fat savings account, being able to work your own hours, being your own boss, calling your own shots, and doing your own thing. The ability to fund ministries, enroll your kids into private school, double your tithe, etc.

hook. A customized argument that promises the fulfillment of a new recruit's individual desires.

levels. This refers to the position recruits are automatically assigned once they join. A higher level is only attained by increasing the downline. Three levels would includes (1) you, (2) your recruit, and (3) their recruit. Some MLM companies pay only six levels deep; some more and others less. The fine print usually ensures they won't have to pay as many levels as expected.

multi-level marketing (MLM). A system of distributing a product or service directly from the manufacturer to the consumer, whereby average people—regardless of education, background, race, or financial status—have an opportunity to earn part-time income or even make a career change. Individuals can sign up as a distributor, consultant, or PR representative. They may also sign up other distributors and earn a commission on the product that they purchase. There is typically a small amount of money to be made by selling the product (i.e. buying at wholesale and then selling to someone else at retail). A large amount of money can be made by building an organization of distributors and earning a small percentage on the dollar volume they generate.

opportunity meeting. A large gathering where testimonials are given about the MLM product or business. Often a presentation is made that paints a grim future for anyone in corporate America or a traditional small business. Someone usually explains the compensation plan and questions are asked, "What could you do with an extra $250, $500, or $1000 a month?" Instructions for signing up and getting to the highest level are given, and attendees are made to feel like fools if they don't see the big picture and jump right in.

rallies. Single- or multiple-day events usually starting with dinner, fellowship, and an opportunity meeting. A full day of training from inspirational speakers usually follows, along with recognition for those who've "made it." The entire event is then summed up in a meeting where people can make a smart business decision to "get saved".

upline. This includes anyone who is on a higher level in the organization. The upline earns a percentage of whatever money the downline makes for the business. So they definitely have an interest in keeping the downline excited and committed to the business.

Suggested Reading

If you're interested in the story of my MLM experiences and my journey out:

Athena Dean. *Consumed by Success.* Mukilteo, WA: WinePress Publishing, 1996.

If you're offended at God or at me for exposing you to the message in this book, offended at someone who took advantage of you, or offended at life in general:

John Bevere. *The Bait of Satan: Your Response Determines Your Future.* Orlando, FL: Creation House, 1997.

If you're feeling intimidated by those around you, especially by those who may not be happy about your decision to walk away from MLM:

John Bevere. *Breaking Intimidation: How to Overcome Fear and Release the Gifts of God in Your Life.* Orlando, FL: Creation House, 1995.

If you're feeling like you're in a wilderness:

John Bevere. *Victory in the Wilderness: Growing Strong in Dry Times.* Apopka, FL: Messenger Press, 1992.

If you're tired of the enemy controlling your life:

John Bevere. *How You Can Shut the Devil's Door.* Orlando, FL: Creation House, 1996.

If you're afraid of losing control but tired of your chaotic, frenzied, and stressful life:

Lisa Bevere. *Out of Control and Loving It! Giving God Complete Control of Your Life.* Orlando, FL: Creation House, 1996.

If you're struggling with learning how to hear God's voice:

Peter Lord. *Hearing God.* Grand Rapids, MI: Baker Book House, 1988.

If you truly want to develop an intimate relationship with God:

John Bevere. *The Fear of the Lord: Discover the Key to Intimately Knowing God.* Orlando, FL: Creation House, 1997.

All these books are available at your local Christian bookstore or by calling (800) 917-BOOK.

If this book has touched your life, please let me know. Your struggles are important to me. I want to pray for you and/or your loved ones. Please feel free to write to me at the following address:

Athena Dean
PO Box 1406
Mukilteo, WA 98275

If you are interested in researching what others are saying about the dark side of MLM, you may want to visit the anti-MLM Web page on the Internet at:

http://home.mpinet.net/jhoagland/webhq.html

To order additional copies of

All That Glitters Is Not God

send $9.99* plus $3.95 shipping and handling to

Books, Etc.
PO Box 1406
Mukilteo, WA 98275

or have your credit card ready and call

(800) 917-BOOK

*Quantity discounts available

NOTE: No profits or royalties from the sale of this book are taken by the author. Instead, they are donated to a number of fruitful ministries.